CRE**A**TIVE
HOMEOWNER®

can't fail color
schemes

CAN'T FAIL COLOR SCHEMES

SENIOR EDITOR Kathie Robitz
GRAPHIC DESIGNER Stephanie Phalen
JUNIOR GRAPHIC DESIGNER Maureen Mulligan
PHOTO RESEARCHER Robyn Poplasky
ADDITIONAL PHOTO EDITING Stan Sudol
EDITORIAL ASSISTANTS Jennifer Calvert and Nora Grace
EDITORIAL INTERN Kealan Bakke
INDEXER Schroeder Indexing Services
COVER DESIGN David Geer
FRONT COVER PHOTOGRAPHY *top right* Eric Roth; *bottom right* Karyn R. Millet; bottom left Dan Epstein; *top left* Bob Greenspan, Stylist Sue Andrews
INSIDE FRONT COVER PHOTOGRAPHY Eric Roth
BACK COVER PHOTOGRAPHY *top* Mark Lohman; *bottom, both* Eric Roth
INSIDE BACK COVER PHOTOGRAPHY Karyn R. Millet

CREATIVE HOMEOWNER

VICE PRESIDENT AND PUBLISHER Timothy O. Bakke
PRODUCTION DIRECTOR Kimberly H. Vivas
ART DIRECTOR David Geer
MANAGING EDITOR Fran J. Donegan

Current Printing (last digit)
11

Can't Fail Color Schemes, First Edition
Library of Congress Control Number: 2007922611
ISBN-10: 1-578011-366-4
ISBN-13: 978-1-58011-366-3

CREATIVE HOMEOWNER®
A Division of Federal Marketing Corp.
24 Park Way
Upper Saddle River, NJ 07458
www.creativehomeowner.com

dedication

This book is dedicated to my family of
incredible artists: Denis, Isaac, Elias, and Haniya who also enjoy
color, and my parents, Ruth and Stanley, who have made my life as
colorful as it is!

acknowledgments

I would especially like to thank Stephanie Phelan for
her brilliant art direction, Kathie Robitz for her expertise and support,
and Dan Epstein, a talented photographer and friend. I would also
like to acknowledge everyone who worked so hard making this book
happen, Benjamin Moore & Company, and all of those who
graciously allowed us to photograph their homes.

contents

adventures in
color

You live in a world of color. Your color preferences are very personal, however. Color combinations with which you feel most comfortable will make up your unique signature palette. Rich, deep hues are serious; upbeat combinations are welcoming; and youthful colors are cheerful. What mood do you want to convey in your home? Your individual color scheme should reflect not only the colors you like but say something about who you are. *Can't Fail Color Schemes* offers a wide variety of color palettes that range from neutral to whimsical and from traditional

to contemporary or avant garde. Some palettes are soft and feminine, while others are brawny and masculine. In each case, you'll find suggestions for accents that will enhance the overall color scheme in a particular room. You'll also find useful general information about what each color means, how lighting affects color, the fun in using metallic paints, and how to accent a ceiling with color. *Can't Fail Color Schemes* should be your take-along guide when you're shopping for paint, fabric, or accessories. You can also use it to take the pain out of choosing a color scheme for the exterior of your house. The point is: find your personal color style, pursue it with ease, and have fun.

Part 1

● ● ● ● ● ● ● ● ● ● ● ● ●

living with
COLOR

from colorless

How rooms look with no color, and how great they look with color

When you look at the colors in your home, do you love them? Do you feel that they are a reflection of your personal taste? Do they make you house-proud? If the answer is no, maybe it's time for a change.

to colorful

Pictured here and on the following pages are examples of how fresh, new colors can bring excitement to boring rooms. The right paint color can make a room feel warm and cozy, bright and sunny, sophisticated, or inviting. You can create any of these moods in a room by selecting the perfect hues. Colors can be soft or strong, whimsical or serious. The colors in a home make a statement about the people who live there. Look at the rooms on the following pages, and think of how your home might come alive by introducing it to new colors.

the meaning of color

Know the psychology of colors—different colors can affect the mood of a room. Choose what you want your rooms to feel like!

Red

Red is the color that stimulates the strongest emotional response. A powerful color, luscious red can be exciting and take center stage in any room design. Cherry red is an energetic color symbolizing romance, whereas earthy brick red has the warmth of an earth tone with an understated, classic look. Deep reds have a traditional feeling of importance and stature, and bright reds impart the feeling of daring adventure. Either way, red will attract the most attention—whether it is used as a wall or an accent color.

Orange

Orange is the color of enthusiasm. Orange can range from bright yellow-oranges to deep terra-cotta and rust. The orange family of colors relays the refreshing feeling of fun and warmth. As a bright yellow-orange, the light-hearted feeling of energetic orange is fun and youthful. Rich oranges can be terra-cotta or darker brick orange, which remarkably share the warmth of an earth tone. Used as a dominant color in your design, light orange can be cheerful and whimsical, while a rich-orange theme can be nutty and comforting.

Yellow

When people think of yellow, they think of sunshine. Bright and enthusiastic, yellow can be an optimistic color that is upbeat and bright eyed. The more delicate, lighter wheat tones can be comforting because of their easy-on-the-eyes subtle hues. Coordinating with almost any other color, soft yellows have a homey quality that makes them easy with which to live. Bright yellows, on the other hand, can have a vibrating intensity that can be difficult on the eyes. Because of the saturated quality of intense yellows, they can make young children agitated if overused.

Green

Green is a comfort color. Relaxing and soothing, green is used in places where people are comforted, whether it is a medical facility or a "green room" where people relax before a performance. Lighter soft greens recall nature and soothing earth tones, while dark greens inspire a more conservative, traditional environment. Although usually considered a color that is calming, new versions of green have a feeling of renewal and youthful enthusiasm. These lime and neon greens are playful and energetic. They are fun and cheerful for the young at heart.

Blue

"True blue" is an expression that describes the qualities of loyalty and honesty. That is the color blue. The color of water and the sky, blue denotes integrity. Most popular in bedrooms, this color can be a cool blue-gray or a baby blue, which is restful and calming. One of the most-popular colors, blue generally has a refreshing sense of tranquility. Although some find darker gray-blue to be somber—hence the term, "feeling blue" —it is most often thought of as a "blue-ribbon" color, implying that it is the best there is.

Purple

Rich, deep purples call to mind luxury and wealth. The color associated with royalty, purple denotes a luxurious sense of sophistication. Rich purples are often used in rooms with a quiet elegance, whereas light purples, such as lilac and lavender, are used to convey a light-hearted or romantic feeling. Soft purples can be more feminine than the richer tones of the color, which can create a feeling of splendor and style when you use it sparingly. Whether a whimsical accent for yellows and oranges or a majestic accompaniment to warm earth tones, purples can set the stage for a room.

Brown

The color of nature and the earth underfoot, brown has the feeling of stability and security. A reliable color that ranges from gentle earthy beige and brown-gray taupe to rich chocolaty brown, this earth tone has a sense of timelessness. A mellow and cozy color, the down-to-earth browns recall the luscious textures of wood and leather. The soft tones can be quiet and conservative, the backdrop to any palette, whereas rich browns give the feeling of balance and strength. With the warmth of cocoa and coffee, browns can be hearty and comforting.

Black

Black is the color of understated elegance. A serious color, black has a sense of strength in design. Used as the dominant color in a room, black presents a sense of power and prestige. Overpowering if overused, ebony black can be the perfect backdrop to contrasting colors and metallic accents. Softened by the use of a deep charcoal color or less-saturated lighter grays, the classic black family will complement any color. However, the stature of true black will always embody the style and class of a black-tie affair.

White

Snowy white is the purest color. Bright white gives the feeling of freshness and purity. Reflecting light, bright white enriches the more colorful tones with a strong contrast. Off-whites can bring in more warmth—creamy and pearl-colored whites have a warm glow, for example. Pastel hues paired with a soft white can be a soothing combination, whereas richer colors look crisp and clear alongside clean white. Whether you're working with the earthier ivory variations or pure bright white, either choice complements the palette with a sense of clarity and freshness.

how we perceive color

Believe it or not, everyone sees color a little differently. What used to be called color blindness is actually a color deficiency. Almost everyone sees some color; it is a matter of how much color they see. About 12 percent of men and 0.5 percent of women have some degree of color deficiency. "Is the traffic light red or green?" "Am I sunburned? I can't see the red in my skin." "That bush has flowers on it? I don't see any!" These are the kinds of things someone might say who has trouble seeing certain colors.

Your eyes have three color receptors, called cones, that give you the ability to perceive different wavelengths of light, which translates to color recognition in your brain. People who cannot see the full spectrum of colors have a deficiency of one or more of these cones. The most common

what do you see?

Here are two examples of how some people see a red bedspread in a colorful room, left, and how others may see the same bedspread differently, right.

If you see pink, doesn't everyone see pink? Not necessarily.

is the inability to see the difference between reds and greens. This is far more common than people realize. A person may be wearing a pink sweater, but her friend sees that sweater as a perfect shade of khaki. The friend does not realize that he is seeing the color differently. When choosing a wall color, make sure everyone is happy with the final choice, however they see it!

What is less common is the inability to differentiate between blues and yellows. Lastly, some people are not capable of seeing any color, only shades of gray. However, this condition is rare. "Color Deficiency" is a condition from birth and is mostly inherited. So remember, color-deficient people can't help what they see—and they don't always know that they see colors differently than others.

the differences

There are three ways that people can be color deficient. An easy way to categorize people's color deficiency is the following: **red-weak**, **green-weak**, or **blue-weak**. Each color-deficient person will perceive the colors in their own way. Here are some examples of what these people see.

color	as seen by the color-deficient
bright red	olive green to yellow to orange
true green	bright yellow to taupe to turquoise
blue/purple	gray blue to brown blue to rust

putting light
on the subject
How lighting affects color in your home

When deciding what colors will look best in any room, remember to keep in mind the color of the lighting in the room.

Different sources of light can affect how a room's colors look and how they make you feel.

An incandescent bulb, which is a common household light source, adds warmth to a room. Simple off-white will appear more golden when it is illuminated by only an incandescent bulb. A stronger yellow room, bright in day-

ABOVE The recessed lighting and pendant fixtures illuminate this airy kitchen.

OPPOSITE Both an incandescent lamp and daylight warm this cozy seating area.

light, will look somewhat softer in the evening when the light bulbs soak up the intensity of the yellow. Deep red will appear to be brick red; blue will look slightly green; and cool gray will seem to be warmer taupe.

The incandescent light that you use for most of your indoor lighting needs is perfect for rooms where you look at and groom yourself, such as the bedroom or bath. Your complexion will appear healthier and more attractive under soft, warm incandescence.

The standard **fluorescent** bulb on the

ABOVE Bedside articulated wall lamps provide soft, shaded illumination here.
OPPOSITE An opaque shade prevents glare from this candlestick lamp.

other hand, adds a cool-spectrum cast, an ultraviolet or blue tinge to the colors in the room. Warm wall colors—yellow, gold, orange, wheat tones—loose their warmth in standard fluorescent light. Yellow appears yellow-green, red looks like purple, and skin-tone has a blue-gray cast. It is as if these colors have been "washed" with a subtle blue overtone.

Because of its unflattering nature, it is generally not recommended for indoors, except for some task lighting. However, newer warm-white fluorescents are truer to natural light and don't have the cold blue cast of the old standard fluorescent.

A halogen bulb gives off a bright white light that closely resembles the qualities of daylight. The intensity of the heat produced by a halogen bulb means that you have to be careful where you place it. However, its crisp light provides excellent task lighting. A compact, low-voltage version of halogen is perfect for accent lighting. Because of the balanced purity of the halogen light, artwork, such as oil paintings, photographs, and sculpture, look true to life within its remarkable glow. Therefore, low-voltage halogen lighting is the perfect choice for museums and art galleries, allowing viewers to appreciate the true colors and textures of what is on display.

The most minimal, soothing light source is candlelight. Nothing comes close to the warm glow of the candle's flame to create a serene atmosphere. Whether it is a lit candelabra next to a

deep soaking tub or a small tea light on your bedside table, warm, glowing candlelight creates a cozy and luxurious mood in any room.

Lastly, consider whether your lighting choice enhances the colors in the room. Your eyes will compensate or adjust for the yellow glow or blue cast in the room, but is the amount of light right for the space? The more-saturated wall

OPPOSITE This hallway enjoys the clarity of natural light from the skylight and the warmth from wall sconces. **RIGHT** Subtle light draws attention to a wall of framed prints. **BELOW** Under-cabinet lights illuminate this work surface.

colors, a deep purple or an intense red, will actually absorb rather than reflect the light, requiring more light to illuminate your room.

On the other hand, lighter colors will reflect light and brighten a space.

You can also make light bounce off the ceiling to highlight its accent color or to add softer reflected light.

It is crucial to incorporate adequate lighting for your needs. Maximize your home's exposure to natural sunlight in order to keep spaces bright and upbeat.

Allowing fresh air and natural sunlight to dapple your home encourages a gentle and quiet feeling. Sunlight, better than any lightbulb, creates a mood of peaceful airiness that cannot be imitated by an artificial light source.

ABOVE Brilliant daylight floods this dining area, making it cheerful and airy. **OPPOSITE** Daylight is imitated and augmented by low-voltage halogen lights.

adding shimmer and shine

Metallic paint can add unexpected pizzazz to a room.

With a subtle reflective quality, metallic paint shimmers. When it's used on a ceiling, it delicately casts its color into a room. Light metallic pearl hues will add overall luminance when they are used on a ceiling. Rather than absorbing the color of the walls, the ceiling's metallic-painted surface subtly reflects light into the room. Because the color comes from above where there is no large furniture or window treatments to block it, the luminance simply glows unencumbered inside the space. Delicate pearl-white and sage-green warm silvers or soft golds will add just the right accent to a room—and they don't have to "match" the other decorative elements, either.

In a formal room, you can capture a

OPPOSITE The textured wall treatment here incorporates a subtle metallic gold.
ABOVE The deep-gold metallic luster on the trim and light-green shimmering walls are a stunning combination in this room.

feeling of elegance with metallic-painted surfaces. Used in the right way, the lighter colors can shimmer with a sense of formality and refinement. The warm silvers, pearl whites, or delicate golds can add a breathtaking look to walls and convey a luxurious and stately ambiance. When the paint is used sparingly—on an

OPPOSITE These purple walls glisten in an otherwise understated room.
ABOVE A checkerboard-patterned bathroom wall plays up the contast between shiny and flat paint for effect.

angled tray ceiling or a fireplace or feature wall, for example—the effect will draw immediate attention. It's a clever way to add color and a bit of drama to a room without overwhelming the space with a hue that is too intense.

The richer, brighter metallic colors have a dynamic and dramatic feel. Metallic navy blues, deep reds, or hunter greens for example, will look intense and profound. With the drama of a theatrical performance, the stronger colors, paired with less-intense decorative elements, can be sumptuous and

exciting. Using these stronger metallic colors in tasteful doses can distinguish your house from all others.

·Certainly the most native use of metallic paints is within a color scheme that is planned to incorporate the colors of nature, including various metal and stone. When a design is conceived around earth tones and natural elements, what makes the outcome successful is texture.

The metallic paints in the earth-tone palette can simulate the texture of a metal. Paint colors that range from coppers, golds, and warm or cool silvers appropriately glow with a sense of the metals that they represent. Combining the warmth of

ABOVE Overlapping metallic golds on the walls create an overall iridescence in this elegant living room.

exquisite details

Decorative moldings will stand out beautifully when you finish them with reflective paints. Architectural trim—whether it is plaster or wood—with a deeply carved profile picks up the light and throws shadows, accentuating the design. In both of these examples, metallic paints intensify the emphasis on the detailing.

the earth tones with the metallic hues, whether they are copper, silver, or gold, bestows a suitable shimmer in a room that has been designed around a natural theme.

In general, metallic paints are the most exciting addition to the world of paints. Used more and more today, they should be considered in terms of their finish— smooth or slightly textured—which is as important as their color.

Metallic paints can be sprayed on or applied with a brush. The spray technique adds a smooth glass-like finish. Brush strokes, on the other hand, produce a more textured, aged appearance.

Both types of finishes can be stunning. Ultimately, it comes down to a personal choice. Whatever that choice may be, you'll get the best result if you don't overuse metallic paint in a room.

decorative trim and molding

Architectural details are the eye candy in your home!

The **decorative trimwork** in each room is an important architectural detail. It consists of trim surrounding the windows, doors, walls, ceilings, and sometimes built-in cabinetry or a decorative fireplace mantel. The paint colors you choose are key to drawing attention to these features.

It is important for **visual contrast** to exist between the flat surfaces—walls, ceiling, and floor—and the decorative

BELOW Wainscot adds architectural character to this dining room.
OPPOSITE Classic trimwork in this hall-way elevates the overall design.

trimwork in the room. That way, the **decorative details** will really stand out.

Houses built before World War II frequently contain the ever-popular stained woodwork, which adds the look of furniture in a room. Classic quarter-sawn, stained oak or the more casual chestnut on the first floor and the less-expensive pine on the upper floors is frequently the case. When these homes were built, this was the way to give them stature and elegance. Years ago, when expensive woods were not available, affordable woods were used with the intention of painting

ABOVE Dark-stained cabinetry adds a rustic ambiance to this kitchen.
OPPOSITE The low contrast of the traditional molding gives this older home understated elegance.

them. To imitate the dark woods, strong **muted colors**—golds, historic greens, or gray-blues—were frequently used on the trimwork, while the walls were a lighter neutral color.

Nowadays people choose to paint the trim with more **vivid hues**. A richer trim color allows the walls to wear a softer color. The trim still gets noticed without having to use a deep wall color, which can be too much for some spaces.

Children's rooms can have a brighter

ABOVE Dark trimwork feels rich and authentic in this Victorian home.
OPPOSITE Simple wall colors help this molding show off the conservative decorative style of an older historic home.

trim, and a soft wall color, allowing the trim to be more playful, matching the soft furnishings. Painting the trim in **brilliant colors** takes on a more juvenile, animated look. (Remember: use muted trim colors to add an **historic or period look** to your home.)

A more contemporary application is to use a trim color that is in the same family as the wall color, only slightly lighter or darker. A lighter-color wall with a slightly darker trim accentuates the decorative elements in the room.

This makes the trim less visible. Generally this style is used if the molding in the room is understated, and you want a sleek appearance. Whatever direction you go, selecting your trim color should be done with great care.

ABOVE Rectangular boxes made with picture-rail molding bring architectural interest to these living-room walls.
OPPOSITE In an elegant kitchen, the elaborate cream-colored crown molding adds a stunning feature.

take it to the top

Ceilings are the fifth wall in a room.

Often overlooked in home design, the ceiling completes the color scheme of a room. If the walls are a warm color, **the ceiling** should reflect that warmth. If the walls are a cool color, the ceiling should reflect either the cool palette or the mood of the room. Homeowners generally think of the room's color as the wall color, forgetting that the ceiling's hue can make an equally important statement. If you

ABOVE Soft lavender adds a decorative touch to this low, slanted ceiling.

OPPOSITE A warm-color ceiling brings coziness into this dining room.

are not selecting a contrasting color for the room's ceiling, you can paint the ceiling to match the trimwork, especially if the trimwork is white, off-white, or a cream color.

OPPOSITE The dramatic tray ceiling brings a dynamic design element into this otherwise simple family room.
BELOW A subtle suggestion of color, the delicate sky-blue ceiling enhances the peaceful mood in this living room.

For an accurate color selection, it is important to remember that the ceiling treatment should match the house style. If the architecture is plain, apply soft colors for an understated look. If the house has strong architectural features—elaborate moldings, wainscoting, and so forth—and rich wall colors, then a beamed or coffered ceiling is appropriate.

When adding **decorative beams** or coffers to a ceiling, remember to match them to the style of the other trimwork.

If the room has painted moldings and trim, the ceiling treatment can also be painted. Stained trim and molding in a room can carry a natural-stained wood-beam ceiling. There is also the option of using **wood paneling** on the ceiling. A wood-paneled bead-board ceiling can cover up any surface imperfections with ease. You can paint the bead board as you would a standard ceiling or stain it to coordinate with the room's other trimwork or molding.

With a dramatic, angular ceiling in an ultra-modern home, a unique treatment is required. Because it attracts the light and throws shadows, which a flat surface does not do, this type of ceiling can be one of the most important design elements in a contemporary home if it is treated with flair. Whether you paint it a bright color, apply metallic finish, or add an interesting texture or pattern to it, the ceiling will be unique and exciting.

BELOW Bold, dark blue adds a sense of drama and makes this room fun for entertaining.

OPPOSITE The bright-green color accentuates the striking ceiling in this contemporary open-plan layout.

A more traditional approach is to simply paint an existing flat ceiling. Remember that the lower the ceiling, the lighter the color; the higher the ceiling, the richer your color options. With a light color, whether it is a white or another delicate hue, you will be less aware of a low ceiling height. If the ceiling is a strong color and only a foot or two above your head, it will be distracting and may make the room feel uncomfortable. On the other hand, a ceiling height of 11 feet or more can make a room seem too tall. So a deeper, richer color will visually lower the ceiling, giving the room a more intimate feeling.

Don't be afraid to go too dark if your high ceiling is very tall. Although such a color selection is dramatic, you will find

OPPOSITE With intersecting beams, this colored coffered ceiling complements the beautiful trimwork in the room.

BELOW The more subtle ceiling color shows off the ornamental ceiling trim.

that it makes a tall room more pleasant.

A richer contrasting ceiling color works well in a room, especially when the room is lacking in architectural detail. Adding a color to the ceiling that draws attention will create more visual interest in the room. When you are looking for the right contrasting color, look at your floor for inspiration. If your carpet is in the sage-green family, perhaps a

BELOW The ceiling and wall color in this dining room picks up the warm tones in the rug. Painting the beams the same color as the trimwork unifies the design.

light green would be a nice touch. If you have an Oriental rug with deep reds, golds, and blues, painting the ceiling a pale gold will add warmth.

In an older home, the ceiling color can also be extended to cover the top portion of the wall down to the frieze.

A newer trend is to make the ceiling a color that is easy on the eyes, not too light or dark. The color of a light-blue sky is the most popular. With the sky-like freshness, a lighter blue can have a tranquil effect on a room.

So choose your ceiling color carefully. It can be a beautiful accent in a room.

Part 2

selecting
YOUR STYLE

warm
and
welcoming

design your home with charming ambiance

It is truly rewarding to know that family and friends feel welcome in your home. The colors you use for the places where you gather can make these rooms comfortable and inviting. Here are some color schemes that you could adapt to make your own home gracious and—above all—welcoming.

details

The glow of lighthearted lavender looks as fresh as summer in these rooms. Accents in warm yellow and rich, earthy orange can make them even more inviting. With a touch of dynamic navy blue for contrast, this palette is the height of drama.

warm yellow

Warm yellow will enhance the natural light in a room and enrich light purple or blue. If you want to add warmth to any of the cool colors of the spectrum, bring yellow into the palette.

orange

Orange is a strong accent color from the family of warm hues. It has a happy quality. Used in an accessory or on a print fabric, orange would brighten both of these rooms.

navy blue

Navy blue accents would look sophisticated with these soft colors. You could use navy-blue matting for framed wall prints or try to introduce it on soft furnishings.

terra-cotta

Terra-cotta can be used as a rich, neutral accent color. Bringing a few touches of it into the bright room above would make the space feel cozy.

taupe

Taupe combines the rustic warmth of a quiet earth tone with the soft quality of richer brown. A color that will blend with almost any palette, taupe enhances this room's glow.

chocolate brown

Deep chocolate brown adds depth to the rest of the colors in this living room. This luscious hue stands out against the light colors on the wall and fabrics.

powder blue

Blue is always a pretty accent color with yellow. The powder blue of the pillow and the lamp base is quiet and gentle, which is perfect for a nursery. You could also pick up the color in quilts or curtains.

cool green

Cool green would provide another delightful accent color in the yellow room above. It would play off the blues and pinks, balancing the variety of youthful colors.

cranberry

While pink adds a feminine touch to a room, deeper cranberry adds a dynamic rosy accent. The stronger color complements the carefree feeling and adds energy to the palette.

details

The curtains and soft furnishings provide the accent colors in this simple room with a peaceful sea blue-green wall. The overall look is that of easy-going elegance.

silvery blue

Silvery blue complements the metallic and glass objects in the room. The accent color could be introduced with other accessories, such as soft furnishings or dried flowers.

coral

The warm tones of coral enhance the palette with hues from the opposite end of the color spectrum. This color tones down the the impact of the blue-green walls.

copper

Rich copper is the ultimate accent color choice if you want to add warmth to a home. Here it appears in the curtain panels and matching pleated shades.

kelly green

Classic kelly green would contrast well with the aquatic color of the wall. It's a color that has the richness and depth to complement the traditional features in the room.

bright red
This spirited bright red brings some fun and adventure into the living room above. As seen on the pillows and window treatments, it energizes the neutral colors.

subtle green
Subtle green adds a gentle dollop of new color into this inviting space. A soft color choice for the wicker furniture and decorative elements, it's a relaxing component in the design.

details

This wide-open room is perfect for entertaining, and the accent colors increase the welcoming mood. Together with the warm-yellow wall color, the touches of red and green look comfortable and friendly.

yellow-beige

This wispy yellow-beige is understated yet delightfully warm and friendly. A quiet color like this is ideal as a background hue for brighter accents.

burgundy

Burgundy is intense, which is why it looks gorgeous as an accent to the subtle yellow-beige. This rich, royal-red hue stands out as the color of the throw on the sofa.

rustic green
Rustic green pairs well with this informal interior. The weathered furniture has a hint of the color, which enhances the casual mood of the family living area.

greenish taupe
A natural color, greenish taupe is a blended earth tone that would warm the room. A spacious environment needs a color like this to make it feel cozy.

royal blue
Inspired by the bright-blue walls, accents in rich royal blue would add a bit of drama to the space. You could bring it in with window treatments or pillows.

slate blue-gray

Slate blue-gray looks classic in the part of the room that is used as a home office. The warm blue portion of the color mixture balances the cool gray component.

summer green

Bright summer green would be a fun accent color to add to the desk. With the brightness of new grass, this shade of green is a cheerful accent in the serious work space.

warm taupe

Warm taupe is an earthy color that would gently soften the work area. It's a comfortable hue that would help tone down the bold, blue wall color.

cheerful yellow

A cheerful-yellow accent wall sets the tone for the room above. The yellow window treatments reinforce the brilliant color, while the ceiling adds a stunning luminance from above.

geranium red

Playful geranium red appears in the print used for the upholstery. It balances the strength of the color on the accent wall and window treatment.

royal blue

Another perfect accent color would be royal blue. This traditional hue adds depth to the palette. The color could be used for decorative elements and throw pillows.

purple
With the informality of cotton fabric, the purple chairs bring a cottage color into this sunlit room. An eye-catching hue, this accent holds its own in an intense palette.

bright green
A clear, bright green is a great accent color for this cheerful scheme. The green bridges the blue and yellow colors in the room. You can pick up this color in the fabrics or fresh flowers.

brick red
The earthy brick red here is a perfect alternative to traditional red. As the ground in the floral fabric on the sofa, it blends beautifully with the warm, rust-color rug.

details

Truly elegant, these rooms painted a pale apple color are inviting because they are warm. Eye-catching from any direction, this color palette looks great during the day or in soft evening light.

metallic gold

A metallic glimmer adds formality and elegance to the room above. Even in small touches, such as in the frame around the painting or the spine of the books, gold gets noticed.

neutral bisque

Richer than tan, neutral bisque is still the quiet color in the room. With wall and accent colors that are dynamic, this comforting hue is the perfect choice.

chocolate brown

Deep and luscious, nothing is as inviting as chocolate brown. It's the color of the pillow and pottery in the room on the opposite page. The contrast it makes with the soft colors is stunning.

neutral ground

design with understated warmth and elegance

Neutral colors are the light and warm earth tones in the palette. Understated and restful, they allow you to bring accent colors into your design that range from the delicate to the fanciful. Decorating with neutrals is easy and the results can be rewarding, whether you use the creamy, pale hues of the palette or the animated "punch" colors.

treatments

These contemporary rooms are classic examples of the neutral, mushroom-color taupe. Comfortable and uncluttered, this simple decorating palette allows the design elements in the room to capture your attention. Contrasting colors can be incorporated in soft furnishings, framed art and photographs, or fresh floral arrangements.

dusty gold

A dusty gold will add warmth to this subdued space. The muted camel-color gold adds a distinctive look. The contrast between the taupe and gold is handsome and appealing.

lavender

Lavender will add a delicate, pleasing touch of color. A sweet lavender-color accent against the neutral walls adds a bit of romance when it's used for floral accents or bed linens.

navy blue

Navy blue is the dynamic accent that adds a strong note to the design. This rich blue can be daring and good-looking. An occasional navy throw or pillow will make your statement.

details

A quiet and subdued environment, this mono-chromatic living room relies on the addition of small, but perfect touches of color to intro-duce classic yet whimsical notes into its restrained design. Brighter colors have been introduced in pillows, accent pieces, and artful elements that are purely decorative.

rich red

A rich red accent looks exquisite in this simple room. Luscious and bold, it makes the strongest design statement. (Remember: the right color is the one that captures your attention.)

bright yellow

The bright yellow adds a spark to this living room. Lending a playful touch as an illuminated accent color on the pillows, it never fails to get noticed in a softly colored room.

orange

Orange is the light-hearted relative of the richer rust color.
Its earthiness combined with its cheerful attitude makes it a
perfect accent color for this serene space.

coffee

A light brown, this coffee color is richer than the deep tone of the
wood furniture. It visually connects the bright accents with the
subtle color of the wall and upholstery.

lime green

Animated lime green adds a joyful touch to a neutral scheme. Used sparingly, it transforms this creamy white room into an inviting place. A moderated splash of this color is all you need.

bermuda blue

The relaxed color of a Bermuda blue sky would beautifully complement this room. A clear, peaceful color, it looks fresh and brings a sense of the outdoors inside.

true green

Olive green is a classic. Adding depth alongside brighter colors, the beauty of a rich green is always captivating. This earthy version is a superb addition to the ivory-white room.

cinnamon

Cinnamon brown is the ultimate warm and cozy color. Softer than traditional dark brown, cinnamon is nutty and satisfying. With a touch of copper, this brown is the perfect "comfy" choice.

pale sky blue

Pale sky blue contrasts beautifully with the bed linens in this room. Whether used on accent pillows or a painted ceiling, sky blue is genteel, light, and airy in contrast to the rich, earthy browns.

midnight brown

Midnight brown is the deep, dark chocolate of the color palette. Rich and luxurious, it adds drama and stature to this bedroom. Used sparingly, this color looks classic and sophisticated.

details

With neutral beige walls, this room's mood is defined by the accent colors found in the furnishings. The beauty of neutral walls is that they give you the freedom to decide specifically where and how you want to add color, whether you introduce it through fabrics, furniture, artwork, or accessories. A neutral background is understated. How you decorate and define it is up to you!

creamy ivory

Creamy ivory is the shade of white that has been used on the trim in this room. It has a warm glow to it that invites the addition of rich accent colors to enhance the room.

tranquil green

Tranquil green is an excellent accent color for this neutral palette. A soft hue, it allows the stunning wood furniture to stand out. Truly a quiet, almost-neutral color itself, green is relaxing in this bedroom.

cranberry

This toned-down red beautifully balances the wall color. It looks soft and subdued here. Easy to accessorize, cranberry, a dark shade of rose, can be sassy and inviting, too.

details

A classic example of how color sets the mood is demonstrated in this cozy space that is both neutral and exotic at the same time. A comfortable living room, the dimly lit space has an intimate feeling that is inviting. The soft furnishings feature a pattern of beautiful colors, while the wall is a classic khaki beige-green. When the wall color is understated, there is more freedom to select colors for the furnishings.

metallic gold

Metallic gold can be the exotic touch in a room. A visual surprise, the shimmering movement of metallic gold will add a luxurious, formal quality to the decor.

muted crimson

Muted crimson adds a cozy contrast to a neutral scheme without overpowering it. Here it lends a vintage feeling to the room that is graceful as well as stylish.

olive green

This is a time-honored hue that gives off a sense of age. Darker than sage green, the deeper version is a true olive color. It adds depth and contrast to this elegant living room.

cordovan

Cordovan is the luxurious cross between deep plum and brick red. Sometimes called "burnt raisin," this dynamic color suggests luxury and complements the neutral walls.

earthy treasures

use earth tones for simplicity and warmth

When combined with naturally warm, earthy hues, certain accent colors can create an irresistibly inviting environment at home. Crossing the lines from classic to contemporary, "natural" colors range from delightful cream to brick red and deep bronze. Selecting the right earth tone will create the look and feeling you want for your home.

special touches

A romantic room that's lavish with charm takes its cue from the background color and the accents. With a warmth and coziness, the overall coffee-color scheme establishes the earthy mood. Accent colors, used sparingly, grab your attention and establish this room's intimate style.

lemon-lime

Cheerful lemon-lime, a delicate version of olive green, is an ideal accent to the other earthy colors. Light olive green is an earth tone with a fresh feel that suggests ease.

peach

A lively addition to this coffee-color room, romantic peach adds a joyful touch. As an accent on soft furnishings or decorative items, the peach hue is femininity with a twist.

mushroom

A rich mushroom color adds warmth to this simple unassuming palette. It provides a strong contrast to the lighter-patterned fabrics in the room, thereby accentuating them.

gold
Warm gold is the perfect cozy accent to these lighter wood cabinets. The blonde color of the stain is heightened by an accent color that shares the same golden touch.

dusty green
Sometimes an earth tone can be restrained, such as dusty green. A relaxing color, this neutral green is subdued and understated in this kitchen.

brick red
A more energetic accent-color choice could be brick red. Spicy and warm, this earthy rust-colored red is a "punch" color that gets noticed.

rich gold

A more classic approach to the room above would be to incorporate an elegant rich gold. It's a dazzling accent color that won't overpower the room's overall design.

coral

A gentler way to introduce a red accent is with coral, which is festive yet soft. A bit whimsical, coral is the ideal color to balance the serious design in the room.

dark green

Accents in dark green, picked up from the tapestry that hangs on the wall, would stand out in this understated room. The rest of the fabrics are neutral and make a texturous fashion statement.

details

This delightful room has timeless appeal, and its serene look is remarkable. The accent colors listed below will enhance the sense of gracious comfort in this low-key living room. Warm and earthy, yet soft, the colors are an important part of the overall mood in this living room.

light blue
A lighter accent-color choice for this neutral space is an airy light blue. With a sense of calmness, the breezy hue would add a happy-go-lucky note to the design.

amber gold
With a rich traditional appeal, amber gold would bring warmth and introduce a bit more formality into the room. Accenting the mushroom-color walls, the gold adds a subtle glow.

green

A soft-hearted green is a pleasing earth tone that is perfect for this palette. This friendly, leafy green blends beautifully with the natural stone colors in the room.

aubergine

With stunning charm, a rich, dark aubergine is the ultimate in visual sensation. A deep, gorgeous accent against the quiet overall scheme, the luscious purple is ideal for soft furnishings.

blue-gray

A cool contrast, muted blue-gray has a vintage charm to it.
A soft and smokey color, the cool silvery gray would stand out
beautifully against the somber colors in this room.

peach

A soothing peach is the ideal accent for this living room.
A more delicate color than rich rust, peach introduces
a warm-hearted touch when it's used for pillows and wall decor.

sienna

A dynamic "punch" color, fashionably rich sienna is the bolder
cousin of the classic brick red. As an accent color, it is a stylish
addition against the room's quieter colors.

rust

The color rust would be luminous in this bedroom.
More intense than the lighter orange hue that has been used, rich
rust has a cinnamon-like sweetness and nutty character to it.

gold

This warm and pleasurable gold looks radiant and feels cozy.
Somewhere between the deeper accents and the pale creamy
colors, this medium tone would capture the eye.

earthy taupe

Earthy taupe would be the ultimate "cuddle-up color" for
this room. Amid the room's existing humble palette, earthy
taupe would add a touch of drama, too.

warm camel

Warm camel is Mother Nature's warmest beige—and it would be a mellow addition to the room above. This natural color blends easily with the other beiges and brown-stone colors in the room.

rosy cinnamon

Adding a touch of romance to an earthy brown room can be done with rosy cinnamon. As a delicate accent color for throw pillows, wall decor, or knitted throws, rosy cinnamon is ideal.

tuscan red

A rich Tuscan red pairs beautifully with natural, earthy colors. It adds a fashionable accent on pillows in the brick-red and cream-color scheme, left.

details

With a simple palette, the traditional Old World character of this room makes it a real treasure, especially with the right color accents. Formal yet inviting, the room's wall color stands out beautifully, enhanced by architectural details and trim.

delicate teal

This delicate, almost humble teal blue is an extremely soft accent color that, by contrast, enhances the warmth of the earth tones in this elegant dining room.

teal blue

Bumping up delicate teal to a full-bodied teal blue complements the earthy brown room beautifully. You can see it on the chair upholstery and in the rug where this vintage hue looks charming.

chocolate brown

Luscious, chocolately brown would be the ideal accent color here. Enhancing the coffee-color wall, the hue would look handsome on accessories or furniture.

peach
A tender peach-color accent would be imaginative in these leafy-green rooms. With a sentimental quality, peach is a natural color that can look fanciful, depending on how you use it.

geranium red
A classic when it's paired with sage green, geranium red is a fun and spirited color. Used in fabrics and on decorative elements, geranium red can look unpretentious and informal.

dark mauve
Dark mauve, which has a period look, would be handsome in either of these rooms. As an accent to these greens, dark mauve evokes Old World charm.

details

These subtle rooms, decorated with the quintessential stone-colored palette, provide the perfect opportunity for accent colors to take center stage. Accent colors can be the most eye-catching colors in a modern room or the natural expression of style in a classic setting.

marigold

A jewel-toned marigold would be a vivacious addition to this understated living room. Bright and sunny, this color would bring a good-natured glow to the decorative elements.

rosy crimson

A rosy crimson—a cinnamon lookalike—is nutty, muted, and somewhat Old World. Use a rosy crimson as a way to warm up a gray-taupe scheme.

light blue

A heavenly color for either of these handsome rooms would
be a serene light blue. Light and luminous, this color would be
a delightful touch in these toned-down, quiet rooms.

black

Black would be a dynamic accent in the bathroom above.
Bold and daring, black has a modern edge. As an accent color,
it has the power to attract attention.

romantic innocence

*decorate with
a sentimental touch*

A dding an air of romance to your home can be done with colors that are poetic and enchanting. They range from charming, comfortable country colors to frivolous and fanciful hues. Remember, you can use color as a tool to define your decor. Take a look at these romantic, colorful rooms, and then imagine the fun you can have in your home.

details

Romantic and luxurious, this main stairwell evokes a feeling that draws you into the home. Allowing the architecture in the room to draw the most attention, the paint and fabric colors delicately complement the banister and wainscoting with subtle, dreamy hues. The balance of soft colors and classic architectural style gives this room an idyllic glow.

florida blue

With sky-like clarity, this Florida blue is an exquisite color. A powdery-soft tone, it allows the crisp white, metallic, wood, and earth-tone picture frames to stand out and be seen.

sage green

This delicious green is a lovely accent color for the delicately decorated hall. On fabrics and flowers, this color is a stunning addition to a space ablaze with sunlight.

lavender

A tender lavender adds a stronger accent color in the form of fresh flowers, but it could be introduced in soft furnishings or tabletop accessories. Lavender brings a sweet touch into the space.

soft green
Soft green is a refreshing accent color, especially in this strawberry-pink dining room above. The palette of pink, white, and green has a light-hearted feeling about it.

burgundy
A deeper version of the pink wall color, burgundy is a more saturated hue. An accent color that can be seen in fabrics and dishes, it is rich in contrast to the country-white furnishings.

antique off-white
Furniture and linens in antique off-white lends a casual, country look to the room. Off-white, meaning not pure white, ties all of the elements of the room together.

plum

Plum can be rich, exotic, and cozy at the same time. Because of its strength, it can blend with neutral colors and serve as a beautiful accent. It complements the golden walls, above, perfectly.

soft green

With sort of a dusty look, the softened green provides a background for the brighter colors in the room. A natural, earthy color, it adds a grass-green freshness with a vintage twist.

raspberry

A rosier version of the rich plum color, this raspberry has a delicate feminine appeal. Used as an accent color for pillows or framed prints, it adds a hint of sweetness.

details

In a cozy room with cottage appeal, the antique-style furnishings, tall wainscot, and soft colors create a true sense of old-fashioned romance. The delicate wall and fabric colors, floral prints, and ruffled fabrics bring together the right combination of colors to complete this charming decor.

cream
Cream is the warmest white. With more depth than bright white, richer cream has the nostalgic feel of days past. A perfect backdrop for deeper colors, it also quietly complements them.

earthy green
The earthy green in this room has a slightly faded, vintage look to it. Attractive and soothing, this quiet and understated color sets the perfect wistful mood in the room.

cinnamon
Cinnamon brings a homey warmth into the scheme. This color has the comfort of a rosy-color earth tone. A dustier version of brick red, it's soft quality makes it even more appealing.

sky blue

A brighter sky blue adds a playful accent to the coral-color bedroom above. Balanced by the crisp, clean white, the blue is blithe and showy as it stands out against the brighter colors.

pale peach

A softer version of the coral walls, this subtle peach would be an easy way to connect the wall color with the soft furnishings. Adding the pastel version restrains the intense wall color.

gray-blue

A dusty gray-blue is a tastefully subdued color for this playful space. It enhances the other palette colors. In strong contrast to the crisp white, gray-blue's depth gives it richness and stature.

coral

A lively coral would add an enthusiastic splash of color to this monochromatic blue room above. Bright and playful, the sweet sherbet color has a luminance that enlivens a room.

pale purple

A more youthful look could be achieved by adding a playful accent color, such as pale purple. Used sparingly, it can be fun on pillows, throws, and furniture details.

ocean blue

A luxurious, deep ocean blue would be a striking accent in this light-blue room. Rich in depth, the royal color would be a perfect complement to the delicate wall color.

details

A friendly space, this illuminated living room has creamy shades of off-white and richer golden colors that set the stage for a cozy environment. Bright and cheerful, the color of the curtains and furniture allow the wall color and accent colors in the room to play an important roll in creating the room's ambiance.

golden yellow

This golden yellow enhances the charming greens of the room and adds vibrancy to the space. The accent color can come from flowers or soft furnishings.

lavender

An inspired accent color, delicate lavender adds a touch of fun to a quiet-color room. Lavender, if it's not over-used, can be dreamy and romantic, adding a touch of sweetness to this sunlit room.

taupe

This deep mushroom color could add a sense of the extravagant to this space. More luscious than the quieter colors in the room, rich taupe is the newest warm earth tone.

details

This whimsical child's room is the ultimate in playfulness. Frivolous and romantic, it plays with colors in the palette, whether you are looking at the clothes in the room or at the child-size furniture. Fun and animated, the colors here are delightful.

purple

This playful purple would embellish the energetic pink on the walls with pizzazz. A dynamic color, purple can be brought into this child's room with bed linens, throw pillows, or wall decor.

sunshine yellow

The golden color of sunshine would illuminate this pretty scheme. As an accent, it can be introduced as a splash of color on upholstery and on light fixtures.

pale green

As added vintage charm, pale green accents painted on the room's delicate furniture are an imaginative way to add color. It could also be picked up in bed linens and wall accessories.

brawny
and
beautiful

*create cozy ambiance
with robust colors*

S electing the right colors to complement a mascucline interior is challenging at times because there are so many strong features in the room. Whether the wall color is neutral or bold, it can make a statement if you select accent colors that bring out its best qualities.

details

When a room is painted a saturated wall color, it becomes cozy. In this space, an intense earth tone, slate, looks comfortable and intimate on the walls. However, it allows the brighter colors of the furniture and wall art to grab most of the attention.

gold
Opposites attract. A brilliant, warm gold, chosen for the furniture's leather upholstery, looks flattering against the cool slate color of the wall.

cherry red
An energetic cherry red is the perfect "punch" color for the contemporary living room. In an avant-garde space with strong design elements, the effect is dynamic.

purple
The color complement to gold, purple is rich and playful. This accent, used sparingly on a pillow, adds another lively color note to the overall palette.

creamy beige

Creamy beige is the one quiet note in this powerful scheme. Pleasing and tranquil, this soft choice adds a gracious accent to the living room's intense wall color and grand architectural details.

wild lavender

The most enthusiastic hues have the qualities of more than one color. Wild lavender, a great accent for this room, shares the femininity of pink and the whimsical nature of lilac.

light green

Light green is a leisurely, carefree color. In the earth-tone family, it is the natural complement to the room's red wall color. In this scheme, light green is a great color for pillows and accessories.

butterscotch gold

This elegant room would be stunning with a golden color touch,
especially one as warm and saucy as butterscotch. A few
decorative elements in the hue would soften the room.

mexican brick red

Hearty and earthy, Mexican brick red is a strong accent hue that
would play up the bold wall color in the background. Use it
sparingly for the most striking effect.

midnight black

The most intense accent color is midnight black. Rich and sultry,
the saturated black is powerful against the soft wheat tones. Black
accents always work well in rooms where there is strong color.

gold

Spicy gold is a great color to add as an accent in a neutral scheme. In this quiet room, warm golden touches would be like a few extra dapples of sunshine.

copper

Copper is a genuinely captivating accent color with a metallic glow. It has the tasteful appeal of a classic red apple combined with earthy warmth.

brownish taupe

A snugly, soothing color, brownish taupe is dusty and understated. It combines neutral gray with coffee brown—two colors that blend beautifully.

buttery cream

An easy-going buttery cream would look mellow in this avant-garde bathroom. Touches of this sweet, cream color would soften the look of the dark cabinetry.

dusty warm gray

Dusty warm gray is a neutral color that remains classic. Without making a strong color statement, this earth-tone would lend a formality to this masculine design.

dark-gray teal

A more saturated blue-gray color, dark-gray teal resembles slate. Used on the floor or in accents around the room, it would enhance this scheme with the depth of the stone's hue.

russet

This coppery hue adds a relaxing element to the cool, masculine palette above. A splash of the color on the bed linens enhances the wood tones in the room.

vintage purple

Vintage purple would be a good color choice to add to this simple room. This rich version of the color would blend well with the charcoal gray on the walls.

straw

Pleasing straw yellow looks mellow in the room above. Easy on the eyes, this delicate choice is the right accent color for pillows or decorative elements.

classic burgundy

Classic burgundy would introduce a spectacular flash of color in this room. It is a sentimental color that looks rich and would complement the muted gray walls.

details

The simplicity of these bedrooms makes it fun—and easy—to select color. The overall palette here is strong. What are your rooms like? What do you want them to feel like? Strong schemes can be simple or complex depending upon how you use color. Several colors can be sophisticated if you choose the right combination.

sky blue

Bringing sky blue into the room, above, is like bringing some of the outdoors inside. In combination with the view from the windows, this airy color is the ideal accent in this open space.

silver taupe

Silver taupe is another warm accent possibility for the muted blue-gray walls. Adding a neutral color makes a room that is sparsely decorated feel cozy.

coral brown

This dusty reddish brown would be another great accent choice for the room. A "punch" color, coral brown can make a strong impression on pillows, throws, and wall decor.

rich brown

A nutty, rich brown is deep and restful, as long as you use it sparingly. As an accent here, it would highlight the wood tones in the furniture and flooring.

details

Well-chosen colors used for decorative elements will stand out against the intense wall color in this bathroom. With beautiful slate tiles and granite countertops, the room already has an established palette to keep in mind, but a few accent colors can be eye-candy in the overall scheme.

aquamarine

Aquamarine blue would be a delightful, airy accent color for this dark room. Touches of this relaxing, cheerful color would lift the mood in this private space.

apricot

Apricot is another upbeat color that would be pleasing here. It would coordinate beautifully with the stone surfaces in this masculine bathroom.

brick red

Brick red would be an exciting accent in this space. Its strength would enable it to stand out dramatically against the intense wall color.

sheer whimsy

go for a light-hearted look

Having fun with color can be an irresistible temptation. These rooms show you how to select delightful colors from a classic, earthy, or cheerful palette. The right choices guarantee an inviting, light-hearted look, whether you are decorating a child's room or a room for the young at heart.

gold
Gold accent is the perfect balance for the dashing wall color here. While the wall grabs major attention, this classic gold hue is used to maintain the elegance of the dining room.

apple green
Light apple green can be a festive note in this happy room. You can introduce it as an accent on dishes or linens, or in a print that is used for the window treatments.

navy blue
The color scheme is so playful that adding navy blue would bring a sense of formality into the room. A dynamic hue, it visually blends with the cool colors in the room.

bright yellow

The strong color palette in the youthful room above can handle bright yellow. It's a pleasing accent that can be introduced on painted furniture or accessories.

orange

Orange is another delicious accent color in this playful room. It's a perfect choice for the linens because orange is complementary to blue, which is the color of the bed.

bermuda blue

In a room with electric colors, Bermuda blue cools things down— just a tad. A soft color, it brings out the best of the brighter colors in the room.

lime green

A youthful color, lime green is the perfect addition to the eclectic space above. It looks lively and amusing in some of the room's fabrics and reflects the brightly colored walls.

hot pink

This tropical color, seen on a pair of wing chairs, is the feminine touch in the whimsical living room. Hot pink is a "punch" color that doesn't take a back seat to the room's strong prints.

earthy gray

A quiet accent color is important for balance in the room. Earthy gray is softer than traditional black and provides a rich background for the room's bright colors.

cranberry pink

Delicate cranberry pink is darling in the dining room above. In a room with a strong wall color and heavy furnishings, this pink accent lightens the mood.

rich lilac

Rich lilac is a romantic accent color for this dining room, where it would complement the gilded mirror frame and the other metallic-gold accessories.

black

Classic and chic, black adds drama to the room. Used sparingly, it is stunning on the lampshades and in the drapery fabric, where it accentuates the cranberry pink.

minty green

Minty green shares the luminance of the wall color, opposite. This precocious color is bright and upbeat in accordance with the room's playful furnishings.

royal blue

Dynamic royal blue is an engaging accent for this color scheme. A winning combination with the cool colors in the room, the royal-blue rug is a knockout here.

bright orange

A few animated bright-orange accents add warmth to the room of blues and green, opposite. On pottery, it pops in the cool room above. Orange is intense and electric, so use it sparingly.

orange

Orange would be a great accent color to use with the yellow tile in the room on the opposite page. It makes a great match with green, too. Notice the stripes on the wall in the room above.

brilliant green

Brilliant green is a playful addition to the whimsical color scheme in this child's bedroom. As the background in the bed linens and on the wall, brilliant green holds its own against the strong yellow.

cranberry red

With a stronger contrast to the yellow than green and orange, cranberry red is the "punch" color in the room. Just enough of this bright pinkish red stands out in the comforter's print.

details

Lively and cheerful, this room is appealing because of the unexpected mélange of colors in the palette. The blending of warm, earthy oranges and cool purples and greens adds a whimsical feeling to this naturally bright room.

lime green

An enthusiastic color, lime green is the perfect accent against these purple walls. Glowing in contrast, it illuminates the richer hues in the playful color scheme.

pinkish purple

Blending with the purple walls, pinkish purple adds a lovely accent to the whimsical color palette. Young and feminine, the hue appears in the fabric that covers the chaise.

orange

The beauty of orange as it is used here is how it complements the purple walls. In the semi-sheer fabric on the windows, it looks delicate and lightens the mood.

deep orange

Deep orange is solid and strong against the room's adventurous colors. It's the richest hue in the palette and anchors the wild and romantic scheme.

details

Using playful colors, especially in rooms where you spend a lot of time, can be tricky. If you choose carefully, the results can be terrific. The playful colors in the carpet runner, left, make a simple stairway exciting, for example. In the classic kitchen on the opposite page, color makes a plain room interesting. The green cabinets and blue pendant lamps add delight to what could have been a standard design.

light green

The decision to paint the cabinets light green moves this room from traditional to playful. With a vintage feel to it, the muted hue is the perfect earthy color for the room.

pool-water blue

A beautiful accent color for a fanciful room is pool-water blue. Clean and bright, it looks young and fresh. Use it on the floor coverings, in window treatments, or on the wall.

terra-cotta rust

This terra-cotta rust has a nutty playfulness that stands out as an accent in a room with mostly cool colors. A dash here and there in linens and pottery looks just right.

royal blue

Royal blue is a "punch" color. It doesn't take much of it to provide a rich dollop of intensity in a room of light colors. The contrast between pale and dark colors can be dramatic.

details

These cottage-style kitchens are the ultimate in folksy fun. The bright colors in these rooms feel friendly and inviting. Don't be afraid to add whimsical accents to your rooms.

light purple

Light purple provides the unpredictable note in the color scheme above. Used creatively as the color of the table, light purple complements the kitchen's sunny hues.

teal blue

Airy teal blue has a capricious, innocent look. You can see how well it plays off the earthy color scheme of the kitchen on the opposite page where it is visible on the walls in the pantry.

geranium red

Folksy geranium red would be an excellent accent color for both of these country kitchens. You can pick up this classic hue in a fabric print or pottery.

chocolate brown

A dollop of chocolate brown would add depth to these fanciful color schemes. This homey color is warm and cozy—perfect qualities for a welcoming kitchen.

peaceful
& soothing

*decorate with tender
touches of color*

Make any room in your home a quiet place to relax and unwind by keeping the color scheme toned down and simple. Lower the volume by exchanging a complex scheme of multiple colors, bright hues, and busy prints and patterns for a calm palette of pastels. Otherwise, limit the colors in the room to just one or two.

details

Muted colors create a serene aura in the traditional interior, left, and the modern space, right. Both of these spaces are elegant and understated thanks to the powdery soft colors that make them special.

golden wheat

This delicate hue is a blend of beige and warm golds. A vintage neutral color, golden wheat complements every hue in both of these rooms.

pale blue

Pale blue is characteristically serene. Picked up from the living room rug on the opposite page, it appears on an accent wall. Above, the color keeps the workspace and bedroom low key.

claret

Small accents of rich claret draw attention to the antique rug in the living room. This luscious color can be a strong element in an otherwise subdued scheme.

brilliant yellow

Brilliant yellow is an eye-catching accent color for a tranquil room, but it should be used in moderate amounts to maintain the quiet atmosphere. The room above is a good example.

lavender

Cheerful lavender pillows and a throw add a bit more color to the quiet bedroom room. This pastel hue looks pretty yet sophisticated within the mostly neutral palette.

light brown

Light brown is a neutral tone with an easy-going warmth. Unassuming, this subtle hue coordinates well with the room's overall color scheme.

light blue
Feminine and delicate light-blue accents would coordinate beautifully with the tranquil tones in the room above. The overall palette conveys the feeling of an early spring morning.

lilac
Lilac is a natural here. It pairs beautifully with the pale-green walls. You could introduce it into this palette with fresh flowers and soft furnishings.

neutral taupe
Understated, neutral taupe is mellow and handsome. It provides balance to the feminine colors in the room and, on pillows, makes the crisp white-slipcovered sofa a little cozier.

details

This room shows off a beautiful palette of warm and cool colors. The overall look isn't showy. It's blissfully pleasant and peaceful. Even the color of the flowers play a part in this setting.

sunny yellow
Sunny yellow is a delightful choice to brighten a room that has a muted wall color. Here yellow semi-sheer curtains filter the sunlight to keep the mood soft.

apricot
Delicious apricot is a comfort color. Used on a pillow and in the curtain print, it's just enough extra color to make this simple scheme inviting.

magenta
The clever use of magenta adds one playful color note to the chair. With a feminine flare, magenta provides an unexpected dash of color here.

pistachio green

A temperate pistachio green makes the bathroom on the opposite page colorful but calm. Keep the color scheme simple in a room where you want to pamper yourself.

mustard

For a vintage touch that does not overwhelm, add a few mustard-color accents to the room above. Keep color contrasts low when you want to create a subtle, relaxing atmosphere.

rich teal

Rich teal is a good "punch" color for either of these rooms. But use it in moderation so as not to break the calm spell. Occasional accents in the tile pattern, opposite, do the trick.

details

The mostly monochromatic scheme in this kitchen helps a busy cook remain unruffled. Rich cabinetry and architectural details provide visual excitement, so the color palette can be simple.

periwinkle

A breezy periwinkle would be a stylish accent color in this classic kitchen. The delicate hue is an unassuming backdrop for the spectacular architectural details.

cinnamon

Cinnamon would introduce a nutty blend of playful orange and earthy brown into the palette. This almost all-neutral room can easily handle more color.

navy blue

A striking navy blue would be exciting as an accent in the room. In fact, it already works a bit of magic as it appears in the backsplash tile. Add more of it with pottery.

butter yellow

Soft buttery yellow is pleasing against the cool colors in
these rooms. Accenting with flowers or one or two small items in
the color is all that is needed.

rich sky blue

Rich sky blue would be a winning combination with the lovely
pale blue. Tone-on-tone color (one color in two different shades)
is always an elegant choice.

neutral taupe

An earth tone would add warmth to both of these schemes.
Neutral taupe is a relaxed color that complements the furnishings
in these rooms.

pistachio green
As delicious as ice cream, light-pistachio green is cheerful and mild in the kitchen above. The white tile and countertops keep the look relaxed.

creamy tan
You could accent this simple monochromatic scheme with laid-back creamy tan. It adds color subtly because it's practically neutral, although there is a hint of yellow in it.

kelly green
If you want an element to stand out in a room with soft color, make it bright. An excellent choice would be playful kelly green, which can be seen accenting the room on the opposite page.

soft blue

Soft blue is an ideal accent for both of these rooms. The color can be upbeat and sociable, but it's not too strong for the times when you want peaceful, relaxing surroundings.

yellow

To brighten up these rooms, bring in a few dazzling yellow accessories. The color will warm up the cool palette. When you want to cool it down again, remove the yellow accents.

warm taupe

Warm taupe complements the blue rooms and makes them cozier. Try it on a solid-color carpet or on pillows. Subtle and mellow, it's a restful, neutral hue.

creamy tan

A tender color accent for these serene rooms, creamy tan has a vintage quality. This classic color embodies tranquility and refinement.

lavender

Adding a sweet lavender hue to quiet spaces will put a smile on your face. Lighthearted and youthful, lavender always looks pretty as an accent to pale blue or green.

blue gray

With period overtones, blue-gray adds a touch of tradition in a room. In either space (above or opposite), it's a classic choice for linens or window treatments.

contemporary style

design with unparalleled
modernistic style

The beauty of working with contemporary design is the wide range of possibilities this style engenders. Selections for walls, fabric, and furniture can range from quiet and neutral to dynamic and colorful. Texture, lighting, and color play equal parts in creating an *au corant* atmosphere. Enhanced by a kindred color scheme, contemporary elements produce a room that's unique and exciting.

summer blue

The crisp clarity of a beautiful summer blue would be the
perfect addition here. Bright and friendly, this delightful hue
would balance the serious earth tones in these rooms.

leafy green

This bright, leafy green has a tender quality. Used for glassware
and linens, the lighthearted color would stand out against the sleek
design of these rooms.

red

Rich red would be a vibrant and arresting accent in these mellow,
contemporary rooms. Used sparingly, this "punch" color would
be the eye candy in the room.

details

This is a remarkable room with a dramatic ceiling and oversized skylights. The right accent colors can add a playful feeling or a sense of sophistication to the kitchen. Which sensibility you want to evoke is entirely up to you.

tangerine

With citrus freshness, tangerine would be a youthful addition to this contemporary kitchen. Bright and cheerful, this color blends the warmth of the woodwork with the colors in the room.

slate blue

The stone color of slate blue would be harmonious with the existing wall color. Blended with the natural light from the skylights, this hue maintains an appealing, earthy quality.

passionate red

The drama created by the high ceiling and skylights provides an opportunity for a color that's just as powerful. Passionate-red accents capture the imagination.

light blue-green

With the cool fluidity of spring water, light blue-green is a captivating accent color. Both of these elegant rooms, with their neutral palettes, would welcome this stunning, fresh-water blue.

copper

With a playful sense of style, a coppery accent color would be a distinctive hue in these open and airy rooms. Rich and unique, this color would complement the neutral colors.

metallic bronze

A metallic bronze accent would be an exotic addition. Bronze is a stunning "punch" color on sculptural elements, decorative tiles, hardware, or wall decor.

blue

In such a masculine color scheme, a splash of brilliant blue would be a delight to the eye. A genteel, light blue would be pleasing on towels, flooring, or decorative elements.

teal gray

A dusty teal gray would add a soft touch to the master bathroom above. This muted hue would enhance the relaxing spa-like atmosphere.

dark red

A trendy dark red would be a dynamic color in this modern room. As a bold accent color, this rich and sensual hue adds pizzazz and style to an otherwise reserved palette.

mushroom taupe

The beauty of this contemporary home is the spacious and airy floor plan. Mushroom taupe would warm up this wide-open room, adding a cozy feeling to the earthy decor.

periwinkle blue

A delicious periwinkle blue would be a brilliant accent color in this avant-garde space. An illuminated hue, this color prevails as one of the most popular.

caramel rust

A nutty caramel rust is an ideal choice to enliven this spacious contemporary room. This color harmoniously blends the light walls and deep accents in the room.

details

In this arresting room, with its daring wall color and modern furniture, it is important to select the right accent colors. With an adventurous overall design, a limited amount of mild accent colors is the way to go.

rosy coral

The perfect choice, rosy coral adds a romantic touch to the modern decor. With dark, tailored furniture, this sweet, fruity coral is delicious eye candy in the room.

olive green

A more intense version of the wall color is olive green. Homey and organic, this rich green welcomes additional accent colors that are bright and pure.

yellow

With dazzling freshness, sunlit yellow would suit this palette perfectly. Brilliant and clean, yellow is a ray of sunshine in a room with dark, heavy furniture.

rich coral

For a more intense red accent, bring in this captivating rich coral. As an accent color, it's a spicy addition to the color scheme.

salmon

For a light accent, salmon fits in well with the decor above. It's an understated yet warm color that will draw your attention immediately.

minty green

A lighter cousin of the wall color, minty green would add a blast of freshness to the room. Incorporate it with accent pillows, pottery, or an area rug.

chocolate

Soothing chocolate is both sweet and distinguished. An elegant and mature brown, it can be used as an accent for anything from throw pillows to wall decor.

rich rust

Rich rust has the folksy warmth of terra-cotta pottery and is perfect in the dramatic room above. Festive against the muted greens, this earthy hue adds a bit of zest.

crisp peach

A crisp peach accent would be exquisite against these muted upholstery colors. Delicate and lovely, peach would look lighthearted in this spacious living room.

dark olive green

A serious "punch" color for this dramatic living room would be dark olive. The accent would add contrast and depth to the design. It could be part of a fabric print.

details

This mid-century modern hallway's stark contrasts capture the eye. Adding inviting and buoy-
ant colors would create a delicate
balance in the space.

corn yellow

A cheerful accent to the intense olive brown walls could come
from corn yellow. The color would add a congenial feeling to this
stark space. This dainty version of yellow is a pleasing hue.

light blue

A charming light blue would be captivating in this modern room.
Upbeat and radiant, this color grabs attention instantly. It would
be playful in contrast with the room's decor.

yellow-orange

A more exuberant accent color for this neutral space would be
brilliant yellow-orange. Bold and engaging, this glowing hue stands
out dramatically against the powerful colors.

sweet dreams

take a youthful, romantic approach to bedrooms

Creating a delightful bedroom can be a lot of fun. Whether the room belongs to a child or adult, selecting the perfect fabrics and colors can create a truly darling ambiance. Furniture and decorative accessories are important—but the colors, patterns, and lighting are the elements that will truly define the mood of the room.

details

This delightful mint-colored child's bedroom has all the romance you could ever want. The scheme comes together beautifully starting with the wall color and followed by the bedding, window treatment, and furniture. Extra bits of color here and there make the room personal.

canary yellow

Along with the natural light that streams into this nursery all day, canary-yellow accents illuminate the room and capture the cheerful mood. This splendid color is pure joy.

little-girl pink

A contrasting color to the mint green, a touch of little-girl pink adds the romantic note in this color scheme. Youthful, sweet, and dainty, it's used perfectly here.

baby blue

Powdery soft, baby-blue accents bring a breezy freshness into the space. This lovable color, as it appears on the ceiling, suggests a faded summer sky.

dusty Victorian green

Dusty Victorian green on the ceiling, above, is a surprise accent that has a nostalgic appeal. Its effect is soothing and soft in this rosy room.

teal blue

As inviting as a cool summer breeze, delightful teal blue is heavenly paired with pink. It's introduced into this room by a collection of vintage teal-colored pottery.

cherry red

Cherry red is a jaunty accent in this enchanting nursery.
A bright color, it stands out from the delicate hues in the room.
This delicious "punch" color can be seen in the fabrics.

golden yellow

Golden yellow adds a more formal look to the romantic baby room above. Unlike traditional bright yellow, this vintage color is muted and appears more elegant.

coral pink

This coral pink is also muted, which makes it cozier than the traditional little-girl pink that is typically used in a nursery or a young girl's room.

gray-green

Gray-green, another vintage hue, is soft and would be a perfect accent color in this scheme. It might be part of a rug or a print fabric that could be used for the window treatment or pillows.

details

The beauty of this simple room is the way its charming color scheme is played up in a mixture of patterns. Coordinated colors on the window treatment, upholstery fabric, and wall come together and draw you in as if the room is the only place you want to be.

powder blue

A wonderful soft color, powder blue delicately balances the lighter and darker accents in the room. This restful color is as pure and sweet as can be.

mint green

The playful mint green is a great color for a youthful bedroom. It's lively, warm, and unassuming. Used here as a secondary color, it coordinates well with the powder blue.

rich green

The beauty of a rich tone is the way it can enhance lighter colors. This green adds a dynamic contrast to the powder blue and mint green. Together, the result is fresh and elegant.

princess pink

A feminine color in this day-lit room, lovely princess pink
is soft and romantic as an accent to the softer pink wall color
above. It can be picked up in fabric prints or accessories.

lavender

A touch of lavender would be a delightful accent here. This
delicate color can complement any of the other youthful colors in
the rainbow.

baby blue

Baby blue is a tender color that is used in just the right amount
on the windows and in other accessories here. Blue and pink are
classic colors for young kids' rooms.

hot pink

A bright purplish pink, hot pink is an appropriately playful accent for the primary palette above. It looks luminous on the bed linens, but it could appear as a whimsical note anywhere in the room.

neon green

Neon green is vivacious. Its youthful energy makes it a fun accent color in a child's room. Because neon green is very bright, use it sparingly.

kelly green

In this darling room, kelly green would add just enough of a contrast to the other colors to anchor the room. It's a rich, summery color that would be a bold choice in small doses.

leafy green

Leafy green is a tasty addition to this pretty bedroom. It's a natural choice to stand out against the light wall color. It complements the periwinkle accents with a hint of candy-like sweetness.

periwinkle blue

Periwinkle blue changes with the time of day and amount of natural light. A darling choice here, periwinkle blue is a hint richer than the breezy-blue wall color.

details

There are a variety of places in this room to add color. As it is, the simplified palette is careful not to overdue the number of colors and patterns. Fabrics used for upholstery and window treatments, bed linens, and the wall color blend visually. A few perky accents keep the room fun.

creamy yellow

For a soft sunny touch, you could add a few creamy yellow accents to this periwinkle-blue bedroom. This small spark would brighten the room.

rich periwinkle

Rich periwinkle blue has a hint of purple. This more-saturated version of the wall color would capture attention as an accent in accessories, such as pillows.

butter yellow

A buttery bright color would add a delicious splash to the blue-and-white scheme above. Engaging and cheery, butter yellow could be introduced into the room with pillows, throws, or linens.

tangerine

A radiant tangerine would be dazzling here. Glowing and vivacious, orange as an accent color would electrify the simple blue-and-white color palette.

lilac

Mellow lilac is a sweet accent-color choice for this room. It has a hint of romance that is precious. Lilac is always a sentimental favorite in a young room.

spring green

With lemon-lime delight, spring green has a youthful, slightly mischievous look. As the eye candy in the bed linens and accent pillows, it is ever bright and cheerful in this child's room.

citrus orange

Citrus-orange accents illuminate the young and feminine room. Used sparingly, orange becomes the spirited touch that would be perfect in this colorful yet soft setting.

muted pink

In most palettes, there is a rich color to play against other brighter colors. This muted pink is that charming choice here. The friendly hue makes the room cozy.

sunshine yellow

Sunshine yellow adds a bright, warm touch to the room above. The color is festive and playful. As an accent in pillows and throws, it would bring even more irresistibly sunny accents to the room.

lavender

This brilliant lavender is high-spirited and impish. With a youthful ambience, the light purple walls here set the tone for a whimsical atmosphere with yellow and navy accent colors.

navy blue

A beautiful, rich accent color, navy blue allows the brighter colors in the room to really shine. In lively contrast, navy blue adds a traditional overtone to this brightly colored room.

orange

Luminous orange looks delicious in the golden bedroom above. With deep yellow, gold, and rust hues, brilliant orange dances with energy. Use it as a fun accent color.

burnt orange

Burnt orange is the earthy rust color in this vibrant room. With warm colors on the walls and furniture, the deep rust keeps the room cozy and inviting.

brown

Brown has a contemporary feel to it and provides a sophisticated touch for this animated scheme. This nutty-color addition is warm and plush against the brighter colors.

yellow
Yellow is the splash of sunlight in the room above. Bright and cheerful, it adds a lively accent to the cool, traditional blue-and-white color scheme.

seawater blue
A brilliant seawater blue would be a surprise accent in this room. Bright and fun, this refreshing color introduces a touch of teal into the palette.

nautical navy
The rich nautical navy looks classic and plays well with the nautical motif in this room. With white walls and trim, the shades of blue make the beautiful wainscot outstanding.

bold
and
dynamic

*design with an imaginative
and innovative style*

A room with brilliant color is unforget-table. If you want to make a big state-ment with your decor, be a little daring by choosing a bold and imaginative color scheme. Dynamic colors can be cheerful and sunlit or serious and introspective. See which ones suit your personal style.

warm taupe

Subtle warm taupe would be the perfect color to balance the saturated walls opposite and above. With an earthy, vintage feel, this understated color would look good on upholstery or pillows.

black

Black is an intense color that always has style. Use it to make a big statement. Don't be afraid to let it dominate a large piece of furniture or an accessory.

metallic silver

Combined with the saturated colors in these rooms, delicate metallic silver adds a contemporary look. Metallic-silver accents could be introduced with accessories or lighting fixtures.

rosy rust
A cozy addition to the room above, rosy rust is warm and earthy. The perfect backdrop to the sunlit walls, it balances the brighter colors in the room.

blue-violet
As a brilliant accent color here, blue-violet pulls together a playful, enthusiastic interior. It appears mainly in the wall decor and on soft furnishings, including the solid-color ottoman and striped fabrics.

muted gold
Muted gold is a toned-down version of the intense wall color above that adds a rich accent. It appears in the carpet but could also be used in the window treatments.

purple
Truly a dynamic "punch" color, purple brings royal flair into the scheme. As an accent, it balances the brightness of yellow so that it's simply cheerful.

brick red
A bold, earthy tone, brick red adds an intimate feel to this green bedroom above. Rustic and cozy, the color pulls from the darkest hue in the brick wall.

sky blue
Delicate sky blue would be an amiable accent color. Its soft, soothing quality is always welcome in a bedroom. You could add it with soft furnishings or paint the ceiling with it.

chocolate brown
This saturated hue would perfectly balance with the intensely green walls. It also picks up on the other rich and warm tones in the room, such as some of the colors in the painting.

bright green

Bright green is the perfect companion to both the bold blue of the walls and the deep violet of the chairs above. The color adds excitement to the modern decor.

deep violet-blue

Deep violet-blue grounds this color scheme. Violet is a natural accent choice for color schemes using either of its parent colors, red and blue. Simply coordinate the intensities of the colors.

sweet salmon

Sweet salmon is a good "punch" color for this scheme when it's used in small doses. On the opposite end of the color spectrum from blue, it complements the overall palette.

yellow

Playful yellow animates the saturated rust-color room above. On throw pillows and upholstery, it brightens the room. Touches of it also appear in the painting and the decorative screen.

light green

This crisp light green brings another bright note into the warm palette. It's used sparingly on a pillow and in the screen, but it stands out within the overall design.

details

With the warmth of clay pottery, this stunning brick-red room has a color scheme that is both vibrant and friendly. With a rich wall color contrasted with bright yellow, orange, green, and black accents, the room is at once dynamic and lighthearted.

bright orange

Robust bright orange has clarity and crispness. It's also a sociable color, which makes it perfect in a room meant for entertaining. It's compatible with the bright yellow and green accents here.

black

On the rug and furniture, intense black anchors this colorful room. With stunning simplicity, the black adds a masculine touch that pulls everything together with style.

gray brown

A subtle hue, gray brown is the kindest color in the electric yellow-orange room above. A softer counterpart to the dynamic walls, this earth tone provides rest for the eyes.

red

Glamorous red would be an intense "punch" color for this room. This potent color could look ravishing in a print fabric used for pillows or in accessories.

cream

In a room with bold hues, the addition of a light cream color would add a soft, inviting accent in pillows or as the ground for a rug or upholstery fabric.

lavender

As an accent color, lavender looks whimsical. Here it is a pleasant surprise on a chair. Standing out against the electric room colors, the hue is delicate and pretty.

creamy yellow

Creamy yellow is delightful in this intense room. Reflecting the wall color, this versatile, light-cream color can be used anywhere here to tie together the various hues throughout the room.

pale teal

A mineral-blue color, pale teal is young and delicate in this dynamic room. A gentle accent, it demonstrates how the smallest amount of a particular color is still important in a large room.

details

A unique color can be a pleasant surprise when you walk into a room. Chartreuse—a "rediscovered" green—is daring. It has both an earthy and a youthful appeal that is accentuted here by crisp, painted-white trim and molding.

orange

Even a small dash of bold color can be outstanding. Look at how the orange-color gerber daisies pop dramatically in contrast to the green in the bathroom on the opposite page.

dark brown

Dark brown would look rich as an accent to the wall color in either room. It's warmer than black and brings out the best of the earthy aspects of the green.

metallic gold

Metallic gold would be compelling. Add some of its sparkle with accessories such as picture frames or as piping for the upholstered chairs above.

details

Eye-catching geranium red juxtaposes creamy off-white in these rooms. When you have a limited amount of wall space, use it as an opportunity to add bright, animated color.

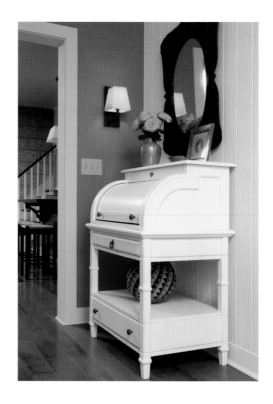

purple

A striking "punch" color for these small spaces would be purple. Without soft furnishings, add accents with floor coverings, wall decor, and small accessories.

muted gold

Adding a warm color to these bright spaces shows their architectural features. Muted gold naturally blends with the creamy color of the painted wood.

dark gray

Dark gray would add a rich but softer mood in these vibrant spaces. The color has a vintage quality that, with the red, looks folksy and charming.

exuberant
and
spirited

vibrant color can make a room exciting

Rooms with joyful colors make you feel good. The secret to using them tastefully is balance. Vibrant color schemes can be exciting—when you know how much is enough. Afraid of overdoing it on your own? Look at the examples here for the right amount of inspiration.

hot pink

Hot pink—even the name of this color has pizzazz. Feminine and wild, it's a knockout on the upholstery in both of these rooms. If you want to use hot pink sparingly, pick it up in throw pillows.

apple green

Both of these homes incorporate high-spirited apple green into the scheme. Flamboyant color looks avant garde in relationship to the conservative architecture.

periwinkle blue

Periwinkle blue contrasts dramatically with the bright colors. Rich and royal, the color adds contemporary style to the interiors of these two vintage homes.

deep orange

Deep orange is a convivial color. On the tablecloth and curtains in the brightly painted yellow dining area above, it enhances the social mood.

bermuda blue

A dashing accent of cool Bermuda blue is a perfect foil for the other hot colors. It's an easy-going color that suits the informality of the space.

black

Using black accents in a yellow room always produces dynamic results because bright colors glow against it. You could introduce it as a "punch" color in accessories.

lemon-lime
In a room with a multicolor palette, each hue makes its
own statement. For example, lemon-lime holds it own against the
equally energetic accent colors in the room.

tropical rose
Tropical rose has a sassy feel. A rich color in the pink family, this
intense hue is upbeat and cheerful on the chairs and in the print
rug and striped curtains.

olive green
Olive green, as seen in the rug and curtains, has a more classic
feel to it. This strong, rich tone complements the more energetic
colors in the room.

banana yellow

Bright and cheerful, banana yellow could be dazzling in this whimsical color scheme above. Animated and vivacious, it brings warmth into a room with mostly cool colors.

kiwi green

Kiwi green is a happy, bright green. Exuberant in this lively room, the color sets the mood. The colorful upholstery fabric and wall color make this room fun.

light purple

A perky light purple looks almost impish. Featured with green in the upholstery on the opposite page, it helps to lighten the look of the traditional furniture and antiques.

details

Color and pattern make this room great. Selecting accent colors can be fun and creative, especially when you can choose them from fabric prints. With a wide variety from which to choose, you can see how several colors work together. The wall and furniture colors here relate to each other, so the accents are added in pillows, bed linens, and decorative accessories.

pink

Pink adds a feminine touch to this room. You can see it in the room's soft furnishings, as part of the wall decor, and in the upholstery fabric and bed skirt.

minty green

This whimsical color appears in the fabric print. It could also be the choice for the bed linens, throws, and decorative accessories.

claret red

A rich claret red color would be the ideal "punch" color in this room. With more contrast than the delicate hues, this rich color would be dazzling in throw pilllows or accessories.

details

This room is vibrating with color. In an unusual twist, the colors that you see here are predominantly those of the furnishings rather than the wall. What makes such an outrageous scheme work? Choosing the right mix of colors.

luminous orange

Luminous orange is an ideal choice to enhance this playful environment above. This bright, enthusiastic color appears in the flooring and window treatments.

lemon-lime

The most intense color here is lemon-lime, which seems to glow above all of the other room colors. It's radiant and energizing here.

sunlit yellow
On a few throw pillows and the coffee table, sunlit yellow appears
as just a splash of color. Remarkably bright, this hue lights up
against the rich-color sofas.

deep magenta
Brilliant deep magenta looks rich and luxurious on the velvet
sofas. You'll also see it as an accent in the rug. This magnificent
floral color is unrestrained.

colonial yellow

The muted colonial yellow is a soft wheat tone that looks warm and inviting in the intensely purple library above.
A color with a vintage sense, it looks chic here on pillows.

apricot

Apricot has an inviting feeling in this vivacious room.
It's an excellent choice for a room where comfort is key. It's cozy in this setting.

delicate lilac

Delicate lilac would be a dainty accent in this boldly colorful room. This impish hue would be perfect for light-color throw pillows or contrasting wall decor.

rich purple

Dynamic and bold, rich purple is passionate. A richer hue than the wall color, it's royal and classic, which could add to the feeling of luxury in this space.

ocean blue
Delicate in tone, ocean blue provides a peaceful interlude in this bold environment above. Light and cheerful, this color is a pleasing accent in the dynamic and colorful space.

luminous orange
Luminous orange adds a splash of heat. You can see just a tad of it in the rug. Stunning with the complementary blue walls, this fun color glows.

magenta
A brilliant "punch" color, magenta appears on the rug, where it displays a sassy attitude. It's an accent that works well with the other bold colors in the room.

yellow

Vivid colors energize this space. In the home office above (actually, part of a kitchen), bold yellow provides a cheerful, lively environment for work.

royal blue

A carefree royal blue is the eye candy in this room. A truly exuberant color, it shows off brilliantly against the other colors in the room.

orange-red

Orange-red is the most exciting color in this room. Here it's brash and youthful. Cool slate-gray floor tiles keep the overall look down to earth.

details

A wonderful aspect of both of these rooms is the architectural detail in combination with the dynamic colors. Both rooms are playful but classic. With a brilliant blue backdrop, there are many delicious options for adding accent colors.

creamy peach

Creamy peach is a delicate color that would be a good choice for adding a feminine touch to both of these rooms. Lighthearted and soft, it could be outstanding with the dynamic wall color.

lilac blue

Lilac blue is a lighter version of the wall color and has a hint of purple. It's a color that is sweet, charming, and versatile. Use splashes of it in pillows or towels.

grass green

Grass green is crisp and as fresh as spring. It looks blissful against the powerful color of the walls. Linens provide the perfect way to bring in this delightful color accent.

classic elegance

design with timeless yet fashionable colors

Selecting the perfect colors for the classic home is gratifying. Your decorating style may be elegant and understated, or you may prefer something more dynamic. The colors you select will help you define it. Whether they are conservative or bold, the colors you choose can create the traditional, time-honored decor you love if you select them wisely.

details

This gracious entrance hall
has beautiful architectural trim
and molding, classic tile, and
an eye-catching wall color to
gracefully pull all of these elements together. The wall color
defines the mood, so it is
important to get it right. The
perfect accent colors add to
the traditional feeling and
overall attractive decor.

neutral taupe

This is a classic color. Reflecting the shadows on
the white woodwork, taupe incorporates the architectural details
without adding another hue to the palette.

rich teal

Rich teal blue is a darker version of the wall color. By adding a
contrasting color to such a delicate palette, the royal version of
the hue would create a more refined look.

crimson pink

This romantic color adds a feminine touch and brings a stylish
accent into the space. A deeper crimson pink has a charming
quality with an earthy look.

golden yellow

A golden-yellow accent illuminates the quiet, earthy living room above. Yellow with a golden hue adds a warm, glowing touch that makes this traditional-style room extra cozy.

sky blue

Sky blue is a light-hearted accent color for a formal room. Blithe and airy, it balances heavy browns. This light blue would look heavenly in this room.

velvety brown

A dark, velvety brown in this room would look chic and formal. Rich and luxurious, the stunning brown accent can be introduced with pillows, for example.

blue-green

A delicious blue-green beautifully complements the warm earth
tones in the room above. As seen in the throw, blue-green is an
eye-catching accent.

tomato red

The tomato red chosen for the ottoman is a more playful accent
than a classic true red. A strong color, it adds a dynamic splash
to the understated palette in this living room.

creamy tan

Creamy tan is a bright hue that brings freshness into this quiet
space. A charming accent, it can be tied in with any of the
brilliant colors in the room, or it can stand on its own.

classic burgundy

Classic burgundy is an engaging color that brings a stunning accent into this gracious home. The color appears on the stair runner and adds a formal note to the hall.

nautical navy

Nautical navy could be a traditional contrasting hue here. Using a strong splash of it would set off the gold wall color with understated formality.

rich purple

Rich purple accents are another stylish possibility. Used on upholstery or window treatments, this color would make a theatrical statement befitting the home's elegance.

blue-gray

An historic color such as blue-gray would complement this classic room beautifully. This dusty hue has a gentle, vintage feel to it. As a mellow addition, a lighter slate blue would be charming, too.

olive green

The olive green chosen for the upholstery color is a fashionable choice for this style and one that is popular in traditional homes. The hue is deep and rich.

black

A dynamic black adds a contemporary "punch" color to traditional decor. Black makes a powerful statement against the soft, earthy golden tones.

pale green

Pale green is a youthful color that complements the dark woods in the dining room above. As a color for china or linens, this lighter version of the wall color would add a pleasing touch.

golden wheat

Golden wheat is a good-looking accent color for this room. It blends beautifully with the room's main palette of green, and would bring a warm glow into the room.

black

Black would be a handsome, modern addition to the room's palette. A contemporary color, black is a dynamic, sophisticated choice for an accent.

periwinkle blue

Periwinkle is a unique shade of blue. An engaging color, it adds a cottage-like warmth to the classic living room above. This dazzling blue glows against the muted dark-green walls.

delicate peach

Delicate peach would be a cheerful accent in this room of intense colors. Graceful and subdued, it could be used for the room's soft furnishings.

midnight navy

Deep midnight navy is a dramatic alternative wall color that would contrast deeply with the bright-color trim. A darker shade of periwinkle blue would be a stunning accent to this scheme.

sunny yellow

Sunny yellow is a perfect complement to the dining room's summer-blue walls, above. Sunny yellow and summer blue are lively colors that are delightful together.

light green

Light green would provide a subtle contrast to the wall color. You could introduce this fresh accent in the table linens or as a ground color in a rug.

rich copper

In deep contrast to the walls, a rich copper would add pizzazz to this room. As a decorative element, copper accents can be in curtains, dishes, or even lighting fixtures.

cranberry red

A luscious cranberry red would be a charming accent color for the grand living room above. A color seen in the pillows, fabrics, and rugs, this delicious red is a passionate "punch" color.

rich gold

Rich gold is elegant in this formal living room. A versatile color, gold can be on fabrics, such as window treatments, trim on pillows or upholstery, or brass accents as decorative elements in the room.

charcoal gray

Charcoal gray adds the opulent feeling of black but as a softer, vintage version. It looks striking in this brightly colored room. Gray is a plush accent color.

salmon rose
A softer version of traditional red, this rosy color is an excellent choice for the upholstered bench above. Beautiful and soft, this accent carries a vintage warmth that embellishes the decor.

light-hearted blue
A touch of this light-hearted blue looks darling in a "serious" room. Youthful and attractive, this cool color would complement the neutral earth tones in the room above.

rich caramel
Rich caramel in the rooms above and opposite adds an earthy warmth. With understated elegance, this color creates the perfect balance among the brighter colors.

rich green
With traditional elegance, rich green is a colorful earth tone to add to this room. Already in the green-gold family, the existing palette would get an extra boost from this color accent.

warm taupe
Adding a warm taupe lets the flashy gold take center stage. As a neutral color, warm taupe can be the understated accent that enhances the fabrics and the wood tones.

navy blue
Navy blue would add classic style to this library. It has a richness and depth that strikes the right note on soft furnishings in a traditional decor.

Part 3

• • • • • • • • • • • • •

outer
CHARM

traditional glory

This wood-shingled home with wooden louver shutters is an example of Colonial Revival style. It has an ornate front entrance that features the classical architectural elements that were popular during the eighteenth century and are still today. The color scheme brings out the best in the architecture and remains true to its period references.

red

The traditional, red front door draws you into this home like an inviting smile. The splash of color makes the entry the focal point of the front of the house.

jet black

Elegant jet-black shutters are in stark contrast to the stained-wood siding. Black is the preferred accent color for a classic colonial, and it matches the wrought-iron lamps and railings.

creamy yellow

Creamy yellow would be a delightful accent color for the masculine color scheme. The soft hue would add a light touch to the decorative details, such as the porch spindles.

sky blue

An alternate accent color could be sky blue. Painting the porch ceiling with with this cheerful color would lighten the mood of the somber-gray shake siding.

classic burgundy

Classic burgundy would be a striking color for the porch floor and would bring out some of the architectural details, such as the banister and wood moldings.

mustard gold
This historic hue is a warm accent for the brick-red home above. Mustard gold is best for contrasting lighter trim against a strong body color.

neutral taupe
Neutral taupe highlights the trim around the windows and balances the home's bold color palette. It's a good choice for accenting the small architectural details.

jet black
Jet black is a dynamic color for details. Here it makes the shutters look elegant and adds a sense of grandeur to the front door. Black urns planted with lush ferns soften the entry.

tomato red
A tomato-red color would be a cheerful addition to the naturally graying, shingled house above. Use fit on the thinnest trim and on the front door to create curb appeal.

green-black
A bold green-black is the ideal color for theshutters. This distinctive color has the appeal of rich forest green blended with jet black. This is truly an avant-garde choice.

cranberry red

Brilliant cranberry red would look delicious accent with the understated gray palette above. You could pick up the color in the shutters or front door, or in seasonal flowers.

rich navy

Navy blue is another pleasing choice to pair with the siding. This rich color has a sense of history and style. Use it for an elegant effect on thr shutters and window boxes.

blue and beautiful

When it comes to choosing a house color, you probably can't go wrong with blue. Its many shades can range from deeply dramatic navy to comfortable midtones or whispery pastels. Some shades of blue are European-inspired, while others are all-American favorites. Select the one that best suits your house.

bright red

As American as apple pie, red, white, and blue belong together.
For a playful yet classic color scheme, use bright-red paint on the
front door or plant red flowers in the front garden.

dark brown

Dark brown would be a beautiful accent color on the house above
because it would coordinate with the natural siding and shake roof.
You could paint the trim or the decorative moldings in this color.

details

With a dynamic periwinkle-blue body and green-and-white trim, the colors of this house are charming. Selecting a color as bold as this for a large house has to be done carefully. The balance between the body and accent colors has to be just right.

details

These older homes
have country appeal. Any
version of blue may be
a handsome body color
for your home.

light dusty green
Accents in light dusty green would be ideal for both of these
vintage homes. Use it for delicate decoration or paint the window
boxes with it.

rich gold
Beautiful rich gold would complement the cool tones of the
house colors. A splash of golden warmth could be added by
painting the molding or planting gold-colored flowers.

kelly green
Kelly green is a traditional accent choice for this color palette.
A classic, it incorporates all of the various shades of green in
the garden.

light blue

Light blue would be the foil to this bold wall color. Softening the look on the building, this delicate color could be the choice for architectural trim or window-box accents.

magenta

Magenta is a pinkish red that adds a feminine yet exotic jolt of color. As an accent, it's outstanding against the bright blue of the house above.

brighten it with blue

Summer blues convey a refreshing feeling. The right blue can
create an inviting entrance. Light blue is almost always a good choice for
the front door, columns, or porch ceilings.

rural and rustic

Applying solid-color stain rather than paint will let you add color to the exterior of your house while maintaining the natural look of smooth clapboards or the texture of rough-sawn siding. The palette of stain colors is muted, and because some of the wood texture will show through the finished coat, the result will be rustic, yet refined.

slate blue

A dusty color, slate blue has a charming colonial look to it. Soft and muted, this vintage hue appears delicate against the bolder tomato-red stain on the house above.

dark-gray teal

Dark-gray is a rustic color. Softer than bright green, this saturated hue complements the equally strong body color. Applied to the doors, it makes the garage stylish.

lipstick red

Lipstick red adds a folksy touch to this 200-year-old, charcoal-gray clapboard house. A small amount of the color around the window trim and mullions makes a pleasing difference.

yellow

Adding a splash of yellow enlivens the facade considerably. Introduced by fresh flowers in the window boxes, this bright accent has friendly curb appeal.

soft olive green

The adorable country home above is trimmed in soft olive green. With minimal contrast from this grassy-green siding, the muted palette looks pretty.

midnight green

Rich and dynamic, midnight green is a knockout color for the shutters. This blackish-green hue looks elegant and draws attention to the handsome window trim.

aquamarine

Aquamarine is cool against the woodsy house above. It is the only relief from the deep russet-color of the siding. It's a pleasant surprise to see this color in this type of setting.

butterscotch gold

Butterscotch gold is rich and classic in a rustic scheme. This warm earth tone would provide outstanding shine on the window trim or the front door.

dark brown

Deep and contemporary, dark brown would add formality to this rustic home. It is another alternative for the trim, or it could appear in small accents such as pottery.

mellow yellow

From the palest cream to the most-intense gold, the yellow family offers a broad range of possibilities for the exterior of your home, whether it is a cozy bungalow or a modern Bauhaus style. A touch of this mellow color on the exterior will give your house soul.

lavender

A delicate shade of lavender looks charming with yellow. It blends easily with the blue door above. Add lavender accents with plants and flowers.

pale aquamarine

Pale aquamarine combines light tones of blue and green. It's a splendid choice if you want to complement a yellow house with a soft color on the front door.

light green

For an accent in low contrast to yellow, choose a shade of light green that is similar to the color of grass. This light green is muted and delicate.

kelly green

Kelly green is a classic color that is ideal for the stately house above. The dark-green shutters stand out beautifully against the traditional, creamy-yellow siding.

deep sky blue

A traditional accent for the buttery-yellow house above is deep sky blue. It is a luminous choice for the porch ceiling, where it exudes old-fashioned charm.

midnight navy blue

Midnight navy blue stands out dramatically against the yellow siding. It is stunning on the shutters and on the walls of the foundation, where it camouflages signs of age.

gray

Simple and elegant, gray looks subtle against the light-yellow house above. This natural-stone color blends beautifully with the shingles and the brick on the lower portion of the structure.

lilac

A playful color like this lilac would add whimsy to the facade. If you are daring, you could use it on the front door. Otherwise, plant a border of lilac-color flowers.

deep purple

Deep purple is a rich, saturated hue denoting royalty. Accenting with this color would be theatrical. A good place to add deep purple without going overboard would be the flower garden.

touches of the sun

Yellow adds the perfect touch of cheer to an exterior. It can brighten a dark entrance, right, or highlight handsome features, such as the pair of garage doors, below.

going green

Green has gained popularity as an exterior house color in recent years. It is a time-honored earth tone that has many variations, but it is always cheerful and pleasing. When choosing this color for your home's exterior, consider the assortment of greens from which you can choose, depending on the style and look you wish to capture.

creamy beige

Creamy beige has a more neighborly appearance on the trim than white, which can be stark. By painting the trim this color, the homeowners have softened the look of the stone facade.

burnt sienna

Burnt sienna accents tie into the rich color of the brownstone on the lower portion of the facade. This earthy color adds to the quaint appeal of the house.

pale sky blue

Accenting the porch above by painting the ceiling pale sky blue enhances the open-air feeling of this outdoor space. It's a delightful surprise for visitors when they approach the house.

purple

A delicious touch of purple adds to the charm of this Victorian cottage. Cheerful and sweet, it pops up in flowers here, but it could appear in architectectural accents, too.

burgundy

Traditional burgundy could be the classic note in this home's exterior palette. As a contrasting shade to green, it's engaging against the softer hue.

warm taupe

Warm taupe could be substituted for the white on the garage door. It easily ties in with the color of the natural-shake roof and the stone driveway.

gold

Gold accents would perk up the garage. An easy way to introduce a few accents in this color would be in the flower bed. Gold-tone flowers bloom from spring through fall.

creamy beige

Painting the window and door trim creamy beige diffused the intense, green body color on the house above for a softer, more approachable look.

brick red

Adding a brighter, earthier accent color for decorative elements is a novel approach. A rich brick red would bring out the natural palette used on the house.

essex green

A more-saturated version of green, this hue contains a black tint. It would bring a more sophisticated look to the facade without overpowering it.

sky blue

A door that has been painted sky blue adds country freshness to the house above. Pick up the color in outdoor seat cushions, and you'll add to the curb appeal.

warm coral

Warm coral is an unexpected but pleasing choice for an accent here. It's a shade warmer than traditional pink. Look for it in accessories such as pottery and planters.

victorian splendor

Few architectural styles have more ornament and detail than that of the Victorian period. Too much was never too much—and that applied to color as much as any other embellishment. Today's interpretation of Victorian decorative style is often more restrained than the original. Nevertheless, using color to the play up the charming millwork and moldings on these houses is too tempting to resist. Some people want to accent every bracket, spindle, and scroll by using many colors. But you can keep it simple, too, and let the details speak for themselves.

details

Victorian details can be absolutely delicious when they are not over the top. Colors can embellish or restrain the moldings on a true or a new "Victorian." These colors show off every pretty detail on the banister and railings on the front porch that is pictured here.

lemon yellow

Lemon-yellow accents on the banister, spindles, and stair risers here look cheerful and contrast effectively with the green to bring out the architecture's pretty embellishments.

terra-cotta

A dash of terra-cotta color adds extra interest to the playful color scheme. Rich and warm, this color stands out against the yellow and dark green.

rich green

A dynamic rich green is an intense color for the fanciful design. This strong earth color keeps the overall palette from becoming too whimsical.

details

This beautiful home stands out as a fine example of Victorian grace and splendor. The restrained use of color enhances rather than over-shadows the structure's magnificent period details.

cinnamon

Earthy cinnamon adds a soft, feminine accent here. It subtly draws attention to some of the home's finest architectural details, such as the dentil molding and the columns.

brown

An elegant rich brown is the "punch" color for this dramatic palette. Stunning against the softer cinnamon and cream tones, it gracefully outlines selected elements.

light green
Lovely light green is a youthful color that was chosen for the body of the house above. It updates the period architecture and provides a light backdrop for the highly contrasted details.

deep green
Deep green on the upper portion of the house draws attention to the fish-scale shingles—an important design feature of this Queen Anne-style Victorian.

gold

This warm hue would complement the body color of the house above. If you don't want to detract from the overall blue-and-white palette, use gold to highlight details in the ornate trim.

purple

Purple can work with a cool or warm palette. Sometimes a playful accent, this lively hue would provide some whimsy as a door color or in plantings around the shrubs.

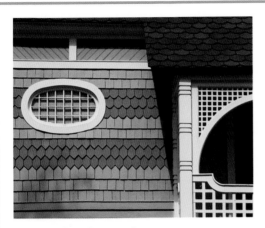

paint it victorian

Victorian architecture features a variety of decorative embellishments. Select colors to show off beautiful details, such as fish-scale shingles and ornate moldings, railings, and brackets.

variety show

When you look at the exterior of your home, make note of its architectural features. Is there one clearly defined style? Even if it's clear that your house is a Midwest Foursquare or a Louisiana shotgun cottage, color plays a big role in defining its character. Although your aim may be to update the house with a contemporary palette, let the original architecture and its time period guide your color selection.

details

These restrained colors are perfect for the restored Arts and Crafts bungalow here. Selecting the right colors for a particular style of architecture or period will enhance its appeal.

warm gray

A restrained warm gray lets the richer accent color take center stage. An easy color on the eyes, this toned-down natural hue serves the Arts and Crafts architecture well.

rich olive

Rich olive is a vintage color that would be a perfect addition to this clapboard house. Its strength would add a depth to the overall color palette.

light green

A slight splash of color makes all the difference to the exterior above. The light-green paint on the window trim makes this architectural feature stand out against the quiet palette.

pale beige

Pale beige appears on the top half of the house. Simple and understated, this color is a conservative choice that has long-lasting appeal.

terra-cotta

The bottom half of the house has been painted terra-cotta. The color of natural clay, terra-cotta is warm and friendly. Together, the neutral colors have lots of curb appeal.

cream

This understated color softens the stucco facade above with paint. Cream closely resembles the original color of the material, but it is more subtle and elegant.

winter blue

Painting the brick on this Tudor-style house makes it an unusual design element. Rich and textural, the winter-blue brick updates the house and draws attention to it.

slate blue

This saturated version of slate blue is handsome on the shutters. This tone-on-tone play of color makes a sophisticated statement that elevates the style of the house.

resources

The following list of manufacturers and associations is meant to be a general guide to additional industry and product-related sources. It is not intended as a listing of products and manufacturers represented by the photographs in this book.

Behr
800-854-0133
www.behr.com
Manufactures paint, varnishes, and related products.

Benjamin Moore & Co.
800-344-0400
www.benjaminmoore.com
Manufactures paint, stains, and varnishes.

Bestt Liebco Corp.
800-523-9095
www.besttliebco.com
Manufactures painting tools, such as brushes and rollers.

Dunn-Edwards
888-337-2468
www.dunnedwards.com
Manufactures paint and related materials.

Dutch Boy
800-828-5669
www.dutchboy.com
Manufactures paint and related materials.

Glidden
800-454-3336
www.glidden.com
Manufactures paint and related materials.

Pratt & Lambert
800-289-7728
www.prattandlambert.com
Manufactures paint, stains, and other related products.

Sherwin-Williams
216-566-2284
www.sherwin-williams.com
Manufactures paints and finishes.

Solo Horton Brushes, Inc.
800-969-7656
www.solobrushes.com
Manufactures artist and utility brushes.

T.J. Ronan Paint Corp.
800-247-6626
www.ronanpaints.com
Manufactures specialty paints.

Valspar Corp.
800-431-5928
www.valspar.com
Manufactures paint, stains, and coatings.

Zinsser Co, Inc.
732-469-8100
www.zinsser.com
Manufactures wallcovering-removal products, primers, and sealants.

glossary

Advancing colors The warm colors. As with dark colors, they seem to advance toward you.

Alkyd paints Paints with artificial resins (alkyds) forming their binder; often imprecisely called "oil-based" paints. Alkyds have replaced the linseed oil formerly used as a binder in oil-based paint.

Analogous colors Any three colors located next to one another on the color wheel.

Chroma See *Intensity*.

Color scheme A group of colors used together to create visual harmony in a space.

Color wheel A pie-shaped diagram showing the range and relationships of pigment. The three primary colors are equidistant, with secondary and tertiary colors between them.

Complementary colors Colors located opposite one another on the color wheel.

Contrast The art of assembling colors with different values and intensities to create visual harmony in a color scheme.

Cool colors The greens, blues, and violets.

Double-split complementaries Colors on either side of two complementary colors on the color wheel.

Earth tones The natural colors of earth; browns and beiges.

Eggshell A thin, brittle semi-matte paint finish.

Glaze A paint or colorant mixed with a transparent medium and diluted with a thinner compatible with the medium.

Gloss A shiny finish that reflects the maximum amount of light.

Hue Synonym for color. Used to describe the color family to which a color belongs.

Intensity The brightness or dullness of a color. Also referred to as a color's purity or saturation.

Intermediate colors Colors made by mixing equal amounts of one primary and one secondary color, such as red-orange and blue-green.

Latex paints Paints that contain acrylic or vinyl resins or a combination of the two.

Nap A soft or fuzzy surface on fabric (such as a paint -roller cover).

Pastel A color to which a lot of white has been added to make it very light in value.

Pigment The substances that give paint color. Pigments are derived from natural or synthetic materials that have been ground into fine powders.

Primary colors Red, yellow, and blue; the three colors in the visible spectrum that cannot be broken down into other colors. In various combinations and proportions, they make all other colors.

Quaternary colors Colors made by mixing two tertiary colors.

Receding colors The cool colors. They make surfaces seem farther from the eye.

Secondary colors Orange, green, and violet; the colors made by mixing equal amounts of two primary colors.

Semigloss A slightly lustrous finish that is light reflective and has an appearance somewhere between gloss and eggshell.

Shade A color to which black has been added to make it darker.

Sheen The quality of paint that reflects light.

Split complementary A color paired with the colors on either side of its complementary color on the color wheel.

Tertiary colors Colors made by combining equal amounts of two secondary colors.

Tint A color to which white has been added to make it lighter in value.

Tone A color to which gray has been added to change its value.

Triad Any three colors located equidistant from one another on the color wheel.

Value The lightness (tint or pastel) and darkness (shade) of a color.

Value scale A graphic tool used to show the range of values between pure white and true black.

Visible spectrum The bands of hues created when sunlight passes through a prism.

Warm colors Generally, the reds, oranges, and yellows; often including the browns.

index

photo credits

pages 1–3: *both* Eric Roth **page 4:** Rob Melnychuk **page 6:** Eric Roth **page 7:** Karyn R. Millet **page 8:** *top* courtesy of Thibaut, collection: Grass Weave/Texture Resource; *bottom* Brian Vanden Brink, architect: Whitten Winkelman Architects **pages 10–11:** *both* Casey Dunn **pages 12–15:** davidduncanlivingston.com **pages 16–17:** Casey Dunn **page 18:** *top right & left center* Anne Gummerson; *center right, top center & center* Eric Roth; *bottom right* davidduncanlivingston.com; *bottom center & top left* Ngoc Minh Ngo; *bottom left* Wesley Rose **page 22:** *both* Dan Epstein, color consultant: Amy Wax/Your Color Source Studios, Inc. **page 24:** courtesy of Armstrong **page 25:** Mark Samu, design: Lucianna Samu Design/Benjamin Moore Paint **page 26:** Mark Samu, design: Delisle/Pascucci Design **page 27:** carolynbates.com **page 28:** Mark Lohman **page 29:** *top* Mark Samu; *bottom* Mark Samu, architect: Robert Storm Architects **page 30:** courtesy of Fypon **pages 31–32:** *both* Mark Samu **page 33:** melabee m miller, design: Judy Collins **page 34:** courtesy of Sherwin Williams **page 35:** davidduncanlivingston.com **page 36:** Eric Roth **page 37:** *left* Jessie Walker, design: Prauss Interior Design; *right* courtesy of Fypon **page 38:** Brian Vanden Brink **page 39:** Brian Vanden Brink, architect: John Morris Architects **page 40:** Jessie Walker **page 41:** Rob Melnychuk **page 42:** Dan Epstein, color consultant: Amy Wax/Your Color Source Studios, Inc. **page 43:** Jessie Walker **page 44:** davidduncanlivingston.com **page 45:** Dan Epstein, color consultant: Amy Wax/Your Color Source Studios, Inc. **page 46:** Mark Samu, design: Denise Maurer **page 47:** Mark Lohman **pages 48–49:** *both* Eric Roth **page 50:** Mark Samu, design: TJK Interiors **page 51–52:** *both* davidduncanlivingston.com **page 53:** Dan Epstein, color consultant: Amy Wax/Your Color Source Studios, Inc. **page 54:** Brian Vanden Brink **page 57:** *top right, bottom right & bottom left* Eric Roth; *top left* Jessie Walker, design: Anne Mitchell Interior Design **page 58:** Jessie Walker **pages 59–60:** *both* Eric Roth **page 61:** Jessie Walker, design: Anne Mitchell Interior Design **pages 62–63:** *both* Eric Roth **pages 64–65:** *both* Bob Greenspan, stylist: Susan Andrews **pages 66–68:** *all* Eric Roth **page 69:** Mark Lohman **pages 70–71:** Eric Roth **page 73:** *top right* Mark Samu; *bottom right & top left* Eric Roth; *bottom left* Joseph De Leo **page 74:** Mark Samu **page 75:** Ngoc Minh Ngo **pages 76–77:** *both* Eric Roth **page 78:** Eric Roth **page 79:** Mark Lohman **page 80:** Eric Roth **page 81:** Joseph De Leo **pages 82–83:** *both* Mark Samu, design: Linda Correia **page 85:** *top right* Mark Samu; *bottom right* davidduncanlivingston.com; *bottom left* Beth Singer, design: NBI Interiors, architect: Angelini & Associates Architects, builder: Christina Tennant Homes; *top left* Mark Samu, design: Jean Stoffer **pages 86–87:** Mark Samu **page 88:** Mark Samu, design: Jean Stoffer **page 89:** Mark Samu, design: Pascucci Delisle Design **page 90:** Brian Vanden Brink **page 91:** Mark Samu **page 92:** davidduncanlivingston.com **page 93:** Eric Roth **page 94:** davidduncanlivingston.com **page 95:** Tony Giammarino/Giammarino & Dworkin **pages 96–97:** *both* Dan Epstein, color consultant: Amy Wax/Your Color Source Studios, Inc. **page 98:** Mark Samu, design: Steve Goldgram Design **page 99:** Bob Greenspan, stylist: Susan Andrews **page 100:** Anne Gummerson **page 101:** Beth Singer, design: NBI Interiors, architect: Angelini & Associates Architects, builder: Christina Tennant Homes **page 103:** *top right* Mark Lohman; *bottom right* Eric Roth; *bottom left* Mark Samu, design: Rinaldi Associates; *top left* Wesley Rose **pages 104–105:** *both* Mark Lohman **page 106:** Jessie Walker **page 107:** Roy Inman, stylist: Susan Andrews **pages 108–109:** *both* courtesy of Waverly **page 110:** Eric Roth **page 111:** Mark Samu, design: Rinaldi Associates **pages 112–113:** Mark Lohman **pages 114–115:** Wesley Rose **page 117:** *top right* Eric Roth; *bottom right & top left* davidduncanlivingston.com; *bottom right* Anne Gummerson **pages 118–119:** *both* Tony Giammarino/Giammarino & Dworkin **pages 120–121:** davidduncanlivingston.com **page 122:** Beth Singer **page 123:** davidduncanlivingston.com **page 124:** Anne Gummerson **page 125:** Tony Giammarino/Giammarino & Dworkin **pages 126–127:** Eric Roth **pages 128–129:** davidduncanlivingston.com **page 130:** *top right* Wesley Rose; *bottom right* Mark Samu; *bottom left* Beth Singer; *top left* Eric Roth **pages 132–133:** *both* Eric Roth **page 134:** Bob Greenspan, stylist: Susan Andrews **pages 135–137:** *all* Eric Roth **page 138:** Wesley Rose **page 139:** Mark Samu **page 140:** Eric Roth, architect: Ben Nutter **page 141:** Thomas McConnell **page 142:** Mark Samu, design: Bruce Nagle, AIA **page 143:** Beth Singer **pages 144–145:** Eric Roth **page 146:** Eric Roth **page 147:** Mark Lohman, design: Dana Jones, The Kitchen Consultant **page 148:** Eric Roth **page 149:** Wesley Rose **page 151:** *top right & top left* Eric Roth; *bottom right* Mark Lohman; *bottom left* Mark Samu **page 152:** Beth Singer **pages 153–54:** *both* Eric Roth **page 155:** Mark

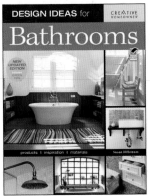